Reflections of You

Donated to

DAWN

By
Barnes & Noble

Reflections of You

Lori J. Olivarez

VANTAGE PRESS
New York

The story is true. The names have been changed.

FIRST EDITION

All rights reserved, including the right of
reproduction in whole or in part in any form.

Copyright © 1998 by Lori J. Olivarez

Published by Vantage Press, Inc.
516 West 34th Street, New York, New York 10001

Manufactured in the United States of America
ISBN: 0-533-12588-X

Library of Congress Catalog Card No.: 97-91172

0 9 8 7 6 5 4 3 2 1

To all my loved ones who supported me along the way

Contents

Preface ix
Introduction xi

1. Childhood — 1
2. Parent Trap — 6
3. No Time to Waste — 9
4. Wedding Bell Blues — 12
5. Saying "Good-bye" — 19
6. Heart and Soul — 26
7. One Simple Mistake — 34
8. Friends Forever — 38
9. Party Time — 43
10. Deadly Desire — 54
11. Bluegrass Fever — 69
12. Truckin' U.S.A. — 73
13. Onward Bound — 78
14. Chicago — 88
15. Back Home — 104
16. My True Love — 109

Preface

Reflections of You shows the resemblance between my life and Rose's life living with manic depression.

Writing this book about Rose's traumas, I was able to relate to the victim as well. It has been therapeutic to help myself overcome the sometimes overwhelming episodes of the past.

If you know of anyone else who has been suffering from manic depression, I suggest you let them read this book. Sometimes just reading about someone else in the same boat sends messages of comfort to someone else in a time when the person who is suffering just needs to know that someone else really cares about them.

Without the prayers and care of others along the way, I may not still be here today to share with you in this special way.

If you can forgive others along the way, and they can forgive you, the battle is won, as far as I am concerned. It takes a lot to admit when we also are wrong.

Please forgive me, everyone, but I had a feeling that the public needed to know once and for all.

You may think that I lost along the way, and in a way, I did, but everything that was lost will come back to me in the end.

Just as Rose chose Rex as her true love along the way, I have chosen the Lord Jesus to be my true love through it all!

May the glory of what we have both learned along the way be given to God!

Introduction

Reporter: Rose Rios, may I have a few words with you at this time? I'm from CZN Broadcasting. Is it true that you are a recovering victim of the following: child abuse, incest, wife abuse, rape, criminal injustice, and a train wreck?
    Rose: Yes, that information is correct.
    Reporter: Is it also true that you suffer from manic depression?
    Rose: Bipolar manic depression to be exact.
    Reporter: Could you please explain to our viewers who gave you the strength to endure all of this?
    Rose: The Heavenly Father, the Lord Jesus Christ, the Holy Spirit, and the heavenly angels showed me the way.
    Reporter: Which brings me to another curiosity question. Is it true that you have actually seen the Lord Jesus Christ, as well as the Heavenly Father?
    Rose: Yes, all of this is true.
    Reporter: Have you ever considered writing a book about all of this?
    Rose: I've considered it. In fact, I've even picked out the title.
    Reporter: Which is?
    Rose: "Reflections of You."
    Reporter: So, what's holding you back?
    Rose: The names and places all would have to be changed to protect the innocent.

Reporter: That shouldn't be so hard to do, considering you've already changed your name. If you don't mind, I could write the book with you.

Rose: I'd be delighted! If you've got the time, I've got the dime for a cup of coffee, somewhere by the dock of San Francisco Bay. I'd like to have my husband join us, if that's okay with you?

Reporter: That's fine by me. I'm ready when you are.

With that last remark, the three of us strolled the dock in search of a cozy little coffee shop, reminding Rose of Saugetuck, Michigan, her home state.

Reflections of You

1
Childhood

Rose began reflecting on her past. As a two-year-old, her little lace anklet of her left foot caught on fire. She had walked through the burning leaves surrounding her swing set while her parents raked the other side of the house. It was an accident, of course. After all, what parents in their right mind would leave a two-year-old, unattended while they were burning leaves?

Could it be that when she almost drowned three years later, it was just another accident? This time her Aunt Trudy saw her sandy brown hair floating on top of the water, and she pulled her to safety. Rose was standing by her mother, when she got kicked aside and fell into a sinkhole. Rose called for the Lord's help, when her Aunt Trudy intervened. Needless to say, Rose was forbidden for the rest of the picnic to go near the water.

At age seven, Mrs. Van Dyke made a beautiful Sunday dinner, because her husband insisted. The mashed potatoes were piping hot, fresh out of the oven. When Rose was asked if she wanted any, she tried to withdraw her plate; however, her mother took a hot spoonful of potatoes and threw them at her in rage. When Rose had to be seen by the doctor after a boy in her class jabbed her blistered fingers with his pencil, her mother told her to tell the doctor that it was an accident.

Why not tell the truth? In Sunday School, she was taught that lying was a sin.

Whenever Rose told a lie, she was grounded, not her mother. Mother's mistakes were always "accidents." However, her father had no alibi for the things he had done to her.

At that time, her father was up to his own bag of tricks. He would conveniently take the newspaper to the main bathroom to do his business every time Rose took a bath. He did not use their half-bathroom to do his business; instead, he invaded Rose's privacy.

Her mother had drawn a bath full of bubbles for her, but the minute the bubbles were gone, her shield of protection left her naked, exposing her completely for her father to see. On several occasions, Rose placed her two towels next to the tub, but when she looked for them, the towels had disappeared. Her father would tell her to get out of the tub. He'd play hide and seek with her towels so that she would have to rely on him to provide her with the missing towels, a game he enjoyed playing. He never did this to her sister, Shelly, only to her.

When Rose grew older, she locked the bathroom door so that her father wouldn't be able to get in. This didn't stop her father from coming in to join her—he had a key of his own.

One night while Rose was washing dishes, she noticed a small key hidden in the cupboard. She asked her mother what the key was for. When she found out it was the bathroom key, she immediately slipped it into her pocket. As soon as the dishes were done, she ran outside and tossed the key ever so gently into the huge field of weeds growing beside their house.

After Rose told me that her father was over six feet tall, I could understand why her knees were shaking.

The next time Rose took a bath, she locked the door and sang "Who's Afraid of the Big Bad Wolf?" After all, her father was a big bad wolf to Rose. And just like the three little pigs, she too had outsmarted the wolf.

She could hear her father yelling, "Let me in!"

She had no desire to do so. He had no right to be there in the first place. She had caught the wolf by the tail this time and wasn't going to let go. Little did Rose know that her father had one last trick up his sleeve.

All was not shades of gray in Rose's life, neither was it just a bed of thorns. Being an entertainer, she had a chance to brighten up the retired vets, the children at the orphanage, people who watched parades, and people in Europe as she twirled her baton.

How many children at the age of nine get a chance to go to New York and then off to Europe? It was a chance in a lifetime.

The gruesome hours of practicing and her mother's bragging to her friends gave baton twirling a bad taste in Rose's mouth. She wished she could be normal like the rest of her friends.

Her mother's constant criticism made Rose more and more annoyed . . . until one contest; Rose cut her hair, marched onto the middle of the gym floor, and announced to her mother in front of about a thousand people that she quit.

Thirteen was an awkward age for Rose. She saved her little brother, Ronnie, from certain drowning in the pond behind their house, when his tiny, plastic boat capsized in the middle. Knowing that he couldn't swim, Rose courageously walked out into the murky water and pulled him safely to shore.

Every night before Rose fell asleep, her mother prayed for her father and Uncle Terry to be saved. Rose did, too, and felt that she ought to pray for her own salvation.

As she did, her mother told her that she could also ask for a gift from the Holy Spirit. Rose decided to ask for three gifts—wisdom, guidance, and the greatest gift, love.

She also asked to become a writer, that she could write a book for the glory of God, and that she be protected from any dreaded disease.

The following Sunday, her mother brought her children, including Rose's younger brother, Ronnie, and her younger sister, Sherry, to a Pentecostal church. The music was lively compared to the boring hymns of the Reformed church. When the minister asked if there was anyone willing to receive a free gift from the Holy Spirit, Rose immediately went forward. She was then asked what gift she wanted to receive. She replied, "The gift of love."

It's not every day that this gift is given out. This was something special. She was slain in the spirit. A floating, peaceful, sensation overwhelmed her as she fell to the ground, speaking in a foreign language she knew nothing of.

Could it be that Rose became clairaudient at that time? If she did, she was unaware of the true meaning.

Clairaudience is actually clairvoyance plus audience plus sense four. It's the supposed ability to perceive and understand sounds, often from a great distance, without actually hearing them, according to *Webster's New World Dictionary*. Rose knew nothing of this until she was thirty-four years old. She was considered to be naive by her parents, when actually she had a keen perception of what was really going on.

One hot summer night, Rose was babysitting for the Perkins. After the baby was asleep, a gush of wind blew through the window. Rose was anticipating the horrors of entering high school. Suddenly, she heard a voice speak to her.

"Fear not, for this will be a very popular year for you." Rose quickly ran outside to see if anyone was there. No one was in sight. The stillness of the night cast only her shadow from the moonlight above.

Rose was nominated for Queen's Court in her freshman year.

Another time while Rose was babysitting for her Uncle Terry's kids, she heard the voice again. The voice she heard this time asked questions that were in her own mind.

"Which one would you choose to be in Heaven with you, Travis or Mary?"

"Can't I take both? Why do I have to choose?' asked Rose.

"Just do as I ask, Rose. Which one do you choose, Travis or Mary?"

Rose chose Travis because he was the naughtiest. He was the only boy in the family, and he was Uncle Terry's favorite.

Seven years later, Travis was thrown in jail for misbehavior. That's when he accepted the Lord as his Savior.

The next thing Rose remembered, Travis was riding with his friend, Trevor, and his fiancée, Sheila, when their car flipped over into a steep ravine. Sheila landed in a bush, with a few scratches, and Travis and Trevor were pronounced dead at the scene.

At the funeral, the cops took Uncle Terry to jail for the back child-support he owed.

2
Parent Trap

It was the summer of her fifteenth year, with driver's training on its way. Rather than take time off for a family vacation, she stayed home, while her father worked. Her mother took Sherry and Ronnie to a Christian campground.

Early one Saturday morning, Rose's father called her into his bedroom. She immediately obeyed her father's orders. She knew if she didn't obey, she'd be severely punished.

He wanted to explain the facts of life to her, but instead, he made her lie down next to him. He started out French kissing, then he fondled her body. Rose knew something was wrong when he told her not to let boys fondle her the way he did. She quickly got out of bed, ran across the hallway to her own bed, and slammed the door behind her.

This bothered Rose dreadfully. How could her own father betray her mother like that?

Rose was stripped of her beauty by the thorns her father placed around her.

What a terrible thing he had done. She wanted to run and hide somewhere. The respect and admiration she once had vanished into thin air.

Certainly, she couldn't tell her mother what had happened. It would just make matters worse.

Rose harbored this guilt and pain until she was well into her prime.

Her parents wondered how she came down with manic depression at the age of twenty-five. Is there any wonder? Does severe depression become manic depression over the years if it is not treated properly right away? It most definitely can.

Rose was diagnosed with manic depression at the age of twenty-five, but she didn't find out what manic depression actually was until she turned thirty-three.

She found this out from her current husband, from a pamphlet he picked up, called *Depression: What You Need to Know,* issued by the National Institute of Mental Health.

Depression: What You Need to Know: If you have been diagnosed with manic depression or know of someone suffering from this illness, ask your doctor to get this pamphlet for you. It is truly a lifesaver.

During this writing, I will take the time to share some of symptoms that Rose had and to help clarify exactly what manic depression is.

Manic depression can occur when an individual has suffered from childhood trauma. It can also be genetic.

Rose most definitely felt trapped between her parents. She didn't want her parents to get a divorce, and she didn't want her father to go to jail because of what he had done.

The only thing she could do was pray, and ponder the pain deep inside her, so that nobody would get hurt by it.

Little did Rose realize that these evil deeds would wear her down, that she would suffer the most because of them.

Rose lost respect for her parents and was grounded many times during her teenage years for not obeying.

Rose often wondered why she was always being punished and her parents were free from punishment. Rose later realized that the Lord would punish them when the time was right.

Rose was suffering pain and agony. Every time Rose's mother reminded Rose of what a good father her dad was, Rose choked back the anger she felt toward her father.

Why did it have to be this way? Why did they mistreat her?

Jesus became her friend. She could tell Him how she felt.

3
No Time to Waste

By the time Rose was sweet sixteen, she had already been an entertainer—a baton twirler and a tap, jazz, and ballet dancer.

As Rose blossomed more and more physically, her mother finally saw the light. No more entertaining for Rose.

She became a cheerleader instead. Unfortunately, between games and practice, she no longer had time for other hobbies.

It was a challenging year, to say the least. The swim team asked her to be a time girl at the swim meets. They also gave her a nickname as they shouted out their own cheer while her squad assembled in the middle of the gym during a pep rally.

"Two-four-six-eight, who do we appreciate? Boom-boom!"

She turned fifty shades of red and ran off the gym floor, leaving a trail of tears behind her.

Why did this have to happen to her? Perhaps, she should've been flattered; instead, she was mortified. A full figure with an hour-glass shape is rare for a sixteen-year-old. Could this have been why Rose was so popular with the guys?

Rose was looking for love, not a poke here and there. That's when she met Jack O'Conner. He was different from the other boys she had dated. She met Jack while she was rollerskating with a friend. She actually fell head over wheels for him. Being the gentleman that he was, he kindly helped her back on her feet.

Most definitely, it was love at first sight for both of them. Rose admired him. He was a hard worker at the age of sixteen. He worked for a lawn crew, and he also worked on cars at a gas station. The only difficulty was that he lived in the city and Rose lived in the country. He went to the Christian school, and Rose went to the public school. Jack's family was poor, while Rose's family was middle class. Rose didn't care; after all, she was in love with Jack, not his parents' house. She explained to Jack that material things meant nothing to her. Besides, Jack was very intelligent. She knew that he would be a good provider someday.

They had been dating for a year and a half when Rose became pregnant. This was a miracle, considering the first time Jack visited her. Rose's father came bellowing in the driveway on her brother's little stingray bike, cursing up a blue streak, because Rose had been told specifically that she was grounded. No guests had been allowed when Jack and his friends arrived.

Needless to say, Jack and his friends disappeared. Rose thought for good, but Jack was persistent. Rose was in tears, because Jack was the only decent guy around. Here, her dad shooed him away as if he were some pesky mosquito.

In the course of two years, from the time they started dating till the time Rose found out she was pregnant, the two of them were madly in love.

One would think Rose's parents would have been angry, but they were supportive, and Jack's parents were the angry ones.

Little did Rose know that this was a sin. Sure, she heard of adultery, but neither of them were married at the time. Because it was considered to be fornication, they both had to go in front of the consistory to confess.

The Reformed ministry had Rose confess before them. Her father, being an elder at the time, was not present at the meeting. It was a good thing, because if Rose was provoked, she might have confessed a few more sins, including her father's.

The Protestant Reformed ministry not only had Jack and Rose confess, but they announced it from the pulpit at the next Sunday service, so that everyone in church could point fingers at Jack and Rose.

The only good that came out of this was that one elder in particular also worked for a well-known factory and was able to get Jack hired in.

It's been sixteen years, and Jack is still working there.

What Rose couldn't understand was that a lot of couples her age were engaging in premarital sex but didn't have to confess because they didn't get caught.

4
Wedding Bell Blues

Rose, at least, got to graduate with her class, but Jack finished his credits at night school. Rose took extra curricula classes in word processing to be with Jack.

Jack and Rose planned to be married two days after Rose graduated. None of Rose's friends were invited, only her and Jack's relations.

It was an outdoor wedding with wild daisies around a trellis. June 10, 1978, looked like rain all day.

Her aunt was supposed to sing. However, at the last minutes, she came down with laryngitis. Her cousin Amy sang instead.

As for the rain, it blew over, and the sun began to shine.

Because they had such a small wedding, her parents put a down payment on their mobile home.

Rose and Jack were able to have a mini-honeymoon in Detroit before he reported to his new job at Reel Case, one of the best factories to work for in the whole state of Michigan.

What bothered Rose was that Jack never let her know how much he was making. He was in his own little world and buying everything he needed for his dune buggies.

He never had time for her. He was always in the garage, creating a new masterpiece.

Jack was a good provider. But when it came to the rest, well, he didn't have time.

Jessica Marie was born October 24, 1978, and almost two years later Jana Marie was born, on September 26, 1980.

Rose wanted to help out with the bills by getting a job of her own. She helped out by babysitting in their licensed home. She also coached cheerleading. She coached junior high and high school. The girls she coached in junior high were seniors by the time she coached cheerleading again.

Tryouts went smoothly except for two girls who had tied scores. Her brother liked one of the girls and the other girl's father had been Rose's sixth grade teacher.

It came down to an essay each girl wrote about what cheerleading was all about. They were both good.

Ronda McGuire was new to the school, whereas Julie McDonald grew up and attended the same school all her life. She had been a cheerleader since seventh grade.

What Rose didn't know was that Ronda's dad was an undercover cop.

Great! The coach was the last one to know this vital information. Rose found out the hard way.

She started getting stopped for everything. Tailpipe too low, foggy back window, speeding three miles over the speed limit, taillights looked dim. You name it, she got pulled over for it, and she lost her driver's license.

She had lost her license; the same time, she lost her marriage; the same time, she lost her respect for all mankind.

Her husband came in early from the garage one night. The girls were in bed early for a change. Rose was in the mood for a romantic evening, but Jack was interested only in TV. Rose took a bath, hoping Jack would get the hint. She then asked him to assist her in applying her body lotion; he insisted Rose quit blocking the TV and go to bed. She drowned her sorrows in her pillow. It was obvious he wanted nothing to do with her. That was the last straw. Rose felt she could no longer turn her husband on. If she couldn't turn her own husband on, perhaps she could turn other men on.

Jack and Rose had been married for six years. In the beginning, Rose had high hopes, and she tried to hold onto her household and marriage. But the harder she tried to hold on, the more the marriage unraveled at the seams.

Manic depression can be very gradual. Stress can trigger it. Rose most definitely was under a lot of stress and Jack didn't help matters any. Instead of letting Rose get a new dress for church, he bought four new dune buggy tires for himself. This made Rose furious. She took one of her butcher knives and made a slit in each tire at the rim. Jack didn't notice at first, but when he did, the roof blew off. Rose just snickered under her breath. It felt good to get even for a change.

Rose became more and more depressed every day. She found it hard to get up in the morning with the children. All she wanted to do was sleep. At night, she lay wide awake.

A neighbor friend of hers offered her some pills that would give her more energy during the day, and they would also help her to lose weight. Later on, Rose found out that the pills she had been taking were speed pills. Rose became addicted. The pills gave her the energy she needed, but they also made her edgy and restless.

After Jessica turned three, she was still wetting her pants. Rose couldn't take it anymore. She took Jessica and slammed her head against the floor. This terrified Rose. She knew something was wrong, but what?

Every time her mother called, bragging about what a good husband her father was, Rose became more angry and didn't know why.

Shortly after, Rose began having flashbacks about her father and the things he had done to her as a child. Rose felt as if she were drowning in the middle of an ocean. Her cries for help went unattended; no one wanted to help her.

Rose became furious as her mother tried to run her life for her. She couldn't break the chain that her mother had around her neck.

Rose was in a terrible turmoil, feeling as if she were a tiger in a cage at the zoo, looking for a way to escape.

Her mother finally suggested that Rose should go to see a shrink. Maybe this was the answer Rose was looking for all along.

Rose went with doubts. What did he want from her? This was her first time with a shrink, so she was a little apprehensive.

The doctor was from Pakistan, barely able to speak English, but he diagnosed Rose as manic depressive. Since he didn't explain to Rose exactly what manic depression was, other than a chemical imbalance, Rose didn't take the pills that he prescribed. Besides, she was told that it would make her groggy at first and that she would gain weight. Just what Rose didn't need. After all, Rose was twenty-five, in her prime, feeling fine on the speed.

Rose never went back to that shrink because he didn't do anything for her at all. All he did was listen; there was nothing he did to help her with her problems.

There were times when Jack came in early, but Rose didn't want to bother him, so she would go over to the neighbor's house for a cup of coffee.

Jack may have regretted that night he had chosen to watch TV, but Rose didn't care. After all, he could've said he was sorry, but he never did.

Since Jack and Rose hardly spoke to each other anymore, she made sure the kids were in bed by the time he came in from the garage. Then, she'd make her way to the neighbor's for coffee. It became a ritual. Mary McDoogle never complained, because her husband was always partying with his friends. Mary had two sons the same ages as Rose's daughters. They played together during the day. Rose and Mary took turns watching the kids.

Jack began to protest, but Rose just ignored him. After all, she was home all day watching her kids, as well as babysitting for others to raise a few dollars to help with the budget.

Since Rose was working, Jack didn't see any reason why he should give her any money at all. He complained because he thought that she didn't do anything during the day.

Perhaps he was joking, but Rose considered this to be a knife thrown at her back. How could he say that, when Rose had all the housework done by the time he came home and supper on the table the minute he walked in the door?

Because Jack started acting like her father in other ways, Rose became resentful toward him. Jack wasn't the only one she resented. Her mother kept calling, telling her how to raise her daughters, complaining about the pills Rose took, etc.

This irritated her extremely. Inappropriate irritability is one of the signs of manic depression. It's a part of the mania cycle.

Rose stopped taking the pills in order to make her mother happy. She became more and more depressed.

There are two cycles that are present with manic depression. As we get into the illness a little further, the signs will be explained and made clearer as we go along with Rose on her journey with manic depression.

Rose remembered an accident she had had when driving. A car filled with teenagers pulled out of a parking lot right in front of her, trying to cross the road. Her automatic transmission jammed on impact. Her two daughters were with her at the time. They were crying because they were frightened.

Rose called several times to reach her husband, but he was not available. The wrecker came and helped them and the groceries make it home safely.

When they got home, Jack arrived five minutes later. He never asked how his family was; all he wanted to know was what happened to the car. How insensitive can a person be?

That was Jack for ya. Forgetting all about his family. Only worried about his material goods. This really bothered Rose.

By the time Jana reached three and Jessica turned five, the marriage was falling further apart.

Rose saw her grandmother's death a week before she actually died. She saw her grandmother's image turn black as she sat at Jana's birthday party. At the time, Rose wasn't sure what that meant. Then she found out; while her grandmother was washing her windows, she fell off the ladder into a cement ravine, causing a hemorrhage to the brain. If she had regained consciousness, she would have been as a vegetable.

Grandma specifically told everyone at Jana's birthday, that if someday she could no longer care for herself, she would rather be dead.

An eerie feeling passed over Rose. Did she wish for her grandmother to die? Absolutely not, but she remembered saying a silent prayer that her grandmother's wish would come true. And then it happened. She died while she was in a coma.

After her grandma's death, Rose went to another shrink. This time a female doctor. Again, she was diagnosed as manic depressive, but wasn't told anything about the illness. Rose took lithium until she started gaining weight, then she stopped because she felt better. She thought manic depression was like the flu. No one told her what the symptoms were of the illness she suffered from. What else would she experience with this illness? Rose wanted to know.

5
Saying "Good-bye"

Saying good-bye is the hardest thing to do, especially when children are involved.

Jack and Rose were hardly speaking to each other towards the end.

Rose met a friend while she was attending school. Her name was Kathy, and she was divorced. This turned out to be a new beginning for Rose. When Jack found out that Rose was stripping at a local bar after hours, he still wouldn't give her a divorce—his religion wouldn't allow such a thing. Rose's parents were more upset than Jack was.

Why would she even consider doing something like this? To get even with Jack and her father. Plus, it was a great way to make some extra cash.

For a Christian girl, mother of two children by the age of twenty, this was not appropriate behavior.

Inappropriate behavior is another sign of manic depression on the mania side.

Maybe now Jack would say he was sorry for ignoring her. Maybe now her father would feel some shame and guilt for the things he did to her in the past. Perhaps someone would take note of the pain she felt.

No such luck. They were all in denial. Instead, Rose carried the burden herself. The shame and guilt Rose felt were from the depression side of the illness.

Her mother always thought that she got the manic depression from the speed she took, but that wasn't the case. It came from her father. The longer he stayed in denial, the worse it became for Rose. Why did he have to hurt her so?

Rose's mother kept heaping coals of guilt on her. If only she could keep her thoughts to herself, but she couldn't.

"Look what you are doing to your children! How could you do this to your family? Think of your brother and sister."

Rose didn't care. She was so badly hurt by her father and Jack, that all she wanted to do was lash out at them.

Rose had received a similar lecture when she got pregnant her senior year in high school. Too bad Rose didn't have enough courage to stand on her own back then. She was always blamed, always the one doing wrong, always the one getting into trouble.

She lost her respect along the way. No matter how hard she tried, her mother always cut her down.

Rose met up with the neighbor guy who was single, and they had an affair. Would this be the final straw? She told her husband about it, but it made no difference to him. He still wouldn't give her a divorce.

The more everyone cut Rose down, the more she wanted to run away from it all.

Finally, Rose reached her limit. She had been working second shift at ABC Laboratory. However, one particular night, she was asked to work until 1:00 A.M. because an order hadn't come in yet. She called home, but nobody answered the phone. Perhaps, Jack was sleeping and didn't hear the phone ring.

Rose wasn't too alarmed until she found the front door unlocked and Jack's truck wasn't in the driveway.

Is it possible that he would leave his children home alone at the ages of two and four? That's exactly what he did.

Rose looked around to see if Jack was sleeping or perhaps at the neighbors', but he was nowhere to be found.

Rose went upstairs to check on the girls. Jana was sound asleep, but Jessica was crying.

"I don't know where Daddy is. I'm afraid, Mom. He left us all alone."

"Don't worry, Jessica. Mom is home now. Everything will be all right."

Rose was able to calm Jessica down by holding her in her arms and rocking her until she fell back asleep.

This infuriated Rose to the utmost.

How could he just leave the girls like that?

It was possible that Jack arrived at the local bar where Rose had occasionally stripped in the past, which happened to be a grandiose notion, that Rose had to make her husband so jealous as to cause him to eventually file for a divorce because of her illness.

She had no idea where he was, but this did not give him the right to leave the girls unattended at the ages of two and four. You just don't do that. Anything could have happened.

Rose was patiently sipping on a glass of milk when Jack walked in at three in the morning. As he entered the living room, Rose looked at him with piercing eyes.

"Where have you been?" asked Rose in a stern voice.

"Out looking for you."

"You knew I was working."

Jack lunged forward. Rose took the milk and threw it in his face, then waited for him to attack.

"You witch! I want you out of my house, now!"

He punched her in the jaw, followed by grabbing her and throwing her to the ground and stomping on her back.

Rose then ran quickly to the phone, but Jack tore it off the wall before she was able to call for help.

She ran for the stairs, racing to get her daughters. By the time she started climbing the stairs, Jack was right behind her. The minute he caught up to her, he threw her down the stairs, stepping on her back as she tried to get up.

Rose was thrown out of the house without her suitcase. She didn't know where to go, so she headed toward her parents house, bruises and all.

Her mother opened the door. Rose was in tears.

Her father took one look at her.

"There must have been something you did to deserve this," he said.

Rose just glared at her father. She was so furious that she could've spit in his face, but she restrained herself.

Most definitely, she couldn't stay there.

The following day, she met Kathy at school, convincing her that she needed a place to stay for awhile. Kathy approved, and Rose stayed the night, safe and sound.

The next morning Rose called Jack to see if he'd let her get some of her clothes. He agreed. He was very polite about the whole ordeal.

She immediately rushed out of Kathy's kitchen door, pausing a second, listening to Kathy's words of advice.

"Be careful. He might start trouble again."

"Don't worry, Kathy. Everything will be all right."

After those words, she left. When she arrived, Jack let her in. Maybe he was having second thoughts about the whole ordeal.

Rose packed her suitcase, along with her "precious moments," as well as her wooden rack and wooden mirror.

Rose couldn't carry everything at once, so she left her purse, her precious moments, and the rack and mirror for round two.

When she returned for those items, the door was locked. Rose knew this meant war. She pounded on the door for Jack to let her in, but he didn't.

Rose kicked in the screened door-window, shattering it in a million pieces. Still, no response. Again, she knocked and yelled at the top of her lungs, thinking Jack would hear her and open the door. Nothing happened, so Rose broke the main door with her fists. She was cut up pretty badly, but she didn't care. This time Jack responded.

"Take this, you witch!" And he threw the bag of precious moments at her, from an arm's length away. "And this, you whore!" He hurled the wooden rack at her head, hitting her in the temple, nearly knocking her unconscious. "And this you tramp!" Again, hitting her in the head with the wooden mirror.

He then walked into the kitchen. Rose followed to get her purse. Once inside, Jack kicked her, threw her around, and slammed her head against the wall.

Rose left in shock. Her white rabbit fur coat was saturated with blood. Rose drove to work all bloody and battered, and told them she would not be coming in to work.

That was a mistake. She should have never gone there in that condition, because the next day when she arrived at work, they fired her, saying that she was in no condition to work anymore.

Rose went back to Kathy's house. Kathy took one look at Rose in shock.

"You're going in to work with me tonight."

At the time, Kathy was working for a law firm. She told Rose to talk to one of the lawyers at the law firm. The consultation was free.

Rose felt pale; she felt the blood drain out of her. The room started spinning, and she grew weaker. She also had a splitting headache. She had to get help. Something was wrong.

She walked into the Med station to get help. The lady at the front desk told her to have a seat in the waiting room. As she turned to find a seat, everything went black and Rose was down for the count.

Rose remembered waking up, with people in white clothing all around her. They asked her so many questions that she could barely answer them. Everything was in a fog. They asked if she wanted to press charges against her husband.

"No, there must have been something I did to deserve this!"

That was a big mistake. She should've pressed charges against him, but she didn't.

The doctors stitched her up, took CAT scans and X-rays and released her, telling her that the information would stay on file for two years in case she changed her mind.

Rose made it back in time to go to work with Kathy for protection and to talk to a lawyer to start divorce proceedings. The lawyer explained things to her, but without any money down, he could only refer her to a lawyer who might represent her with no money down.

Rose took his advice, only to find a lawyer who put her on a waiting list of two years or more.

With that advice, she looked at the attorney, with knife-throwing glares and spoke sharply.

"Who's going to pay for my funeral if I don't survive these next two years? Please explain to my children that it was your fault, not mine!"

This was in 1985, the beginning of the recognition of child abuse and wife abuse. Lawyers and crisis centers didn't really want to get involved, neither did they have the knowledge to represent these kinds of cases at that time.

Rose became frustrated as she tried to find someone to help her. No one came to her aid, so she concentrated on making some fast cash, as well as getting another job to secure her future.

Stripping at a night club, was the only way Rose knew would make her some fast cash, so that's what she did. She also contacted a temporary service to get a job.

If only Rose could get a lawyer before Jack did. She would still have a chance at getting custody of the girls.

Rose found out that her parents had taken the girls to live with them for a while. They figured the girls would be safer there in case Jack and Rose got into an argument again.

Rose went to see the girls, but her mother wouldn't let her in. This made Rose furious. She slammed the door so hard on her way out that she busted the window.

Saying good-bye to the girls was the hardest thing Rose had ever done in her life. She cried many tears over it.

6
Heart and Soul

Not only was Rose suffering from grandiose notions, but she was also suffering from, inappropriate irritability. This, too, is a symptom of manic depression.

She was mad at her mother for not letting her see the girls. She was mad at her father for what he said. She was mad at Jack for not letting her have the girls, and she was mad at ABC Laboratory for letting her go.

She went to the crisis center to see if they could help her in any way, but as long as she didn't have the children, there was nothing they could do.

Every time Rose received cash, Kathy asked for more money for lodging and food. This also made Rose angry because she just couldn't get ahead no matter how hard she tried.

Rose also needed reductive breast surgery done because of her back. She had gone through all the testing while she was living with Jack so that his insurance would cover it. When it came time for the surgery, the doctor told her that he couldn't do it because she was in no shape to undergo surgery. He also told her that Jack had cancelled the insurance policy on her.

Why did it have to be this way? Why couldn't he say he was sorry? Why did he have to be so cold? Why did her parents side with Jack? Why did there have to be so much pain? Talk about major depression. Since Rose was a survivor, she didn't let this get her down. She found a job, molding plastic, on the dark side of town.

She also made a few bucks by pawning her diamond. She was doing the best she could with the resources she had.

In the past, Rose had to turn over her money to Jack, but not anymore. Things were looking better for her.

The first night of work wasn't too bad. In fact, Jack showed up, asking her to return home with him. To Rose, it seemed like a trap. She had been too hurt to return to him.

The second night, Rose had car trouble, never making it in to work at all. There must have been a full moon out that night.

Driving along the city streets at 10:00 P.M., Rose noticed a bunch of African Americans standing on a street corner.

Just then, her car died. As she approached the men, she was grateful that they were so willing to help her during her time of need.

It was a rainy, blustering night. The gentlemen told Rose that they lived only a block away. That she could make a phone call from there, that she could stay there until they got her car fixed. Rose agreed, thinking how courteous it was of them to offer a place of refuge in a time of need.

As a little girl growing up, whenever her mother drove through this part of town, she always told Rose to lock her door, as if some boogey man were after them.

Being a little Dutch girl from the country, a trip to the city always fascinated her.

Rose had heard about rape and about drug dealers, but always thought that stuff belonged in New York, not in Michigan.

Certainly, these charming men weren't like that. Or were they?

Once Rose arrived at the house, she was led to the basement, which was remodeled, complete with a bedroom.

She asked if she could make a couple of phone calls, but that request was denied, with promises that her car would be ready any minute.

Little did Rose know that Satan can appear in sheep's clothing. She had always assumed that she'd be able to find Satan in a crowd, not with the gentlemen fixing her car. They seemed too friendly, even though their names were Papa Bear and Hollywood.

It was getting late. Rose wanted to lie down and rest her tired mind. She was exhausted from it all. The minute she lay down, a pair of handcuffs went around her wrists and she was tied down to the bed.

The only light of hope was four pairs of eyes staring at her. She realized that if she closed her eyes, the whole ordeal would be over in no time.

Rose did not want this to happen. She prayed silently for protection from any dreaded diseases, that no harm come to her in any way, and that when the time was up, they'd let her go.

Since Rose had no money to speak of, Papa Bear and Hollywood told her that she would work for them. Selling drugs and strolling the streets became her new job.

The men who picked her up bathed her and fed and clothed her. They treated her right. They didn't pay her cash like the other prostitutes, because she never had sex with any of them.

When Papa Bear asked her for cash, she had none to give.

One day, Rose hitched a ride to a department store. She had no cash, but needed new clothes. She went in the dressing room, tried the new clothes over her other clothes, found a new, long coat, tucked everything underneath, tore the tags off and went about her merry way. She also picked up some expensive jewelry to give to Papa Bear, so that he wouldn't be angry with her. These actions are known as inappropriate social behavior.

When she got back to town, she stopped at the cop shop, telling the detective everything she knew. He simply nodded and showed her the way to the door. He didn't do a darn thing to help her.

Papa Bear was pleased with the jewelry, but he wanted cash instead. So back to the basement she went. This time, men paid at the door to have sex with Rose.

One night while Rose was selling drugs, Hollywood brought her to a warehouse with a blue light shining. When she walked in, she was greeted by a man with a hooded black cape standing by a counter. He asked her what she had to offer and what she wanted. Rose gave up her watch and a class ring, hoping to get something in return. The man at the counter told Rose to knock on the door at the end of the hallway to the left. She did as she was told. When she opened the door, the room contained crates, boxes, two men, and a pile of money. They told her to leave immediately and warned her not to say a word about it.

Rose walked past the guard, noticing the shine from the revolver pointing straight at her. She silently walked by and headed out the door.

Papa Bear and Hollywood were disappointed that she wasn't able to get them anything. Back to the basement she went.

Rose waited patiently to be set free from this life of crime, praying to the Lord to release her from these chains of darkness.

Then it happened. The next morning, Rose woke up, feeling alive, hearing the footsteps and laughter of children through the vents. The handcuffs had been removed, allowing her to venture upstairs. She heard a small child in the kitchen.

"Hello, is anyone up there?"

"I am. Who are you?" The small voice replied.

"My name is Rose. Who are you?"

"My name is Tyler. Where are you?"

"I'm in the basement. The door is locked, and I have to go potty. Can you let me out, please?"

"I can let you out."

She heard Tyler shoving a chair across the room.

"Tyler, is there anyone with you?"

"Just my aunts and sister."

With that, he unlocked the door, setting the captive free. Rose gave him a big hug before she ran out the door and she made her way to the police station.

Once she arrived, she was in a state of hysteria from all that had happened in the last week and a half.

The detective listened to her story once again, and still did nothing. He was happy to receive the information so that he could be in charge of one of the biggest drug busts ever.

Nothing was done regarding her stolen car; neither was anyone arrested for rape or for holding her captive.

Rose even gave proper names, streets, and addresses of where she had been.

Two years later, the city was cleaned up—thanks to Rose, I'm sure.

After talking with the detective, Rose flagged a cab to go tell her parents that she was okay, only to find that her parents would not let her in. They were afraid of what might happen to them.

She ended up taking the cab back to the city. However, when it came time to pay, she was broke.

Where do you think she ended up this time? A) the cop shop; B) on the streets again; C) at her parents a while later; D) back at Kathy's place; or E) back at Jack's place.

If you guessed A, you are absolutely correct.

Rose was thrown in the slammer for not paying the cab fare, but the men who took her car and the ones who raped her went free.

Rose was furious. On top of that, her bond was set for fifty dollars. Do you think her parents would pay for it? Not Rose's parents. A preacher came to her rescue, but that didn't release her.

During the time she was in jail, Jack served her papers to allow him temporary custody of the girls.

This really tore Rose apart. She ripped everything in her jail cell with her teeth, flushing them down the toilet, clogging the entire jail sewer system.

Jack, after serving Rose with temporary custody papers, helped her parents to commit Rose to a psychiatric unit for thirty days against her will.

This made her angry as a tiger in a cage. After all she had been through. People treated her as a criminal, when they should've treated her as a victim of abuse.

No one said anything to her while she was in seclusion. The next thing Rose knew, she was being taken to a psychiatric unit.

Her parents, along with Jack's parents came to visit her. They were the last people Rose wanted to see. She hated them all for what they had been doing to her.

Jack wanted to know where the car was, but Rose had no idea where it could be. She knew where she had been. With that information, Jack was able to find it; it was gutted out in some alley.

When Rose was told she had bipolar manic depression, she had no idea what it was. She had been told it was a chemical imbalance of the brain, which is true. That's all she was told. No one told her what the symptoms were, only that it was a mood disorder. She understood that part of it. After all, anyone would be a little moody in her shoes.

The whole thirty days while Rose was at the psychiatric hospital, she walked around like a zombie because of being very sedated.

Rose was allowed to see her friends. She decided not to see her husband and family anymore.

One day her mother brought the girls to see her for a few minutes. She held them tight and cried her eyes out.

She couldn't understand why she couldn't raise her children as a good mother should. Raising her children in a loving environment just wasn't possible with Rose and Jack.

Somewhere along the line, love had vanished. Would they ever be able to rekindle the flame they once held for each other?

After Rose completed her thirty days, a hearing came up, and she was sentenced to another thirty days in another psychiatric hospital.

How could they do this to her? Rose was beside herself with grief. Jack refused to have her come home to him. And her parents refused to have her come to live with them.

This made Rose want to seek revenge all the more. How could they be so cruel?

She finally made arrangements of her own to stay at her girlfriend Linda's house for a while.

She was able to get a small job, riding her bike twenty miles round trip to a screen-printing business. It was hard, but she managed.

7
One Simple Mistake

Before continuing with Rose's life, it is well to take note of a few facts.

First of all, her father and mother made mistakes, Rose made mistakes, and Jack made mistakes.

Rose wanted forgiveness, but all they gave her was a few more logs on the fire.

She grew up in a family where there weren't any hugs. Her marriage was the same, because Jack also grew up in a family without any hugs.

No matter how good or how bad times were, the cold shoulder approach was still there.

Even though Rose walked away from the Lord, he never left her side. He carried her through the fire of evil to higher ground.

Each case of manic depression is different from another. Rose carried the weight of the world on her shoulders. In other words, if everyone was stealing, Rose easily fell into this trap, too. Because her judgment was poor, she didn't discern herself from others. Poor judgment is also a symptom of manic depression.

For example, if your *will* is *ill*, you are unable to function as a *whole* human being, unless, you have the right combination of medication to help you.

Rose thought manic depression was like the flu. As soon as the symptoms went away, you were better. Little did Rose know that once you were diagnosed with manic depression, it stayed with you a lifetime.

Upon entering the second psychiatric hospital, she noticed things were different. There was no seclusion for not obeying the rules.

At the first hospital, Rose had worn hand-me-down clothes that were too big for her. Rose had on a man's shirt. She had tucked it in and had rolled up the sleeves before she entered the lunch room. Upon entering, Captain Black stood there giving her the evil eye.

"Wear your shirt the right way, or don't enter."

Rose rolled down the sleeves, which hung down to her knees, and replied to the captain.

"There. I hope you are satisfied."

Captain Black just glared.

"Don't get cocky with me, young lady! Nurse, take her to seclusion until she calms down and respects her elders."

Rose was so thankful that there was no seclusion at the second hospital.

There were activities: group therapies, outings, and crafts to pass the time away.

Jack was more receptive than before. Her parents weren't so judgmental. Still, neither of them would allow Rose to live with them.

When Linda came to pick her up, Rose was more than ready to leave.

A couple of weeks after Rose moved in, just after she started her new job, she went to the department store with Linda.

Rose didn't have any money to speak of, so she slipped a belt around her waist and scissors in her purse. When it came time to check out, she was arrested for shoplifting.

Inappropriate social behavior had just taken place.

Oddly enough, it was the same store her mother worked at during the time they were there.

Could it be she was seeking revenge toward her mother for admitting Rose to the looney bin without her permission?

Needless to say, Rose ended up in jail again. Only this time, she behaved herself. Her mother bailed her out, and she moved in with her parents; then Jack asked her to come back to him.

Rose accepted the invitation graciously. In the back of her mind, she knew she needed her breast-reduction surgery done, as well as a car to get her to and fro.

Rose had prayed to go back home to start things with a brand-new beginning.

Rose and Jack went to a marriage counselor, but all they did was fight. It just wasn't working.

Even their lovemaking included Rose being tied up and handcuffed. This reminded her of the rape, which made her angry and hostile. She had never seen this side of Jack before.

He also held her captive in a closet and wouldn't let her out until he was ready. This aggravated Rose to no end. She became irritated. This was torture all over again. Jack just smiled in a sick sort of way.

Rose endured the pain and suffering just as she had before. She knew that once she received her surgery and her car was fixed, she'd be gone. It was just a matter of time.

Rose stopped taking her medication, because it made her drowsy and it also made her gain weight.

Her surgery was a success, and her car was fixed. The only thing she needed was a job to help her pay the rent.

She got a job at a local diner as a waitress. Which was where she met Harry, who was a jeweler.

He had an eye for Rose and a placed called home.

Each manic depressive episode is different from another and grows worse as time goes on when the patient is not on their medication. You will see the difference by traveling along with Rose throughout the rest of the book.

8
Friends Forever

Harry was in search of a girlfriend, but Rose was in search of a friend to help her escape.
Rose and Jack decided to go uncontested along the way to a friendly divorce. Once the papers were signed, Rose was free to go.
It wasn't any easier to say good-bye the second time around, although this time, there was no broken glass. Rose packed her car full of her belongings, kissed her girls, and said good bye to Jack.
She moved in with Harry for a short time until she found another way out.
Rose met a girl named Kayla Runner. They worked together as waitresses at the local restaurant.
It just so happened that Kayla was looking for a friend to help her pay the rent. Rose was looking for a new roommate as well. Kayla and Rose put the deposit down on a slightly used mobile home in a run-down trailer park that rented out mobile homes.
Rose had gotten a good deal of contact paper to do their home. It went from tacky to wow-this-place-looks great.
In the midst of the run-down park, their home stuck out like a diamond. It was warm and cozy on the inside. They each had a room of their own.

Rose and Kayla were high-class ladies, waiting for their Prince Charmings to take them out of their poverty.

During the time they lived together, they were invited to several outings. For instance, the time they went spoonin' in Saugetuck.

Rose would always bring her spoons (three silver ones). While Kayla played her castanets. They played along with the band underneath the table. People would surround their table just to hear them play. It was great to get everyone involved.

Kayla and Rose shared hard times as well as good times. Like when they got hit in a shopping plaza parking lot. They hit a patch of ice and spun around and were struck by an oncoming car. Rose stayed in the car when the police arrived. Kayla got the ticket for not having her car under control because the lady cop was a friend of the driver who hit them.

Later, Rose wrote a witness letter regarding the scene of the accident, therefore, dropping all charges against Kayla.

One night, Rose and Kayla went to a country bar on the outskirts of town. While they were spoonin' they met up with two gentlemen who asked them to come over for a nightcap.

It was during a blinding snowstorm. However, the two men led the way, with one in front and one behind them.

Good thing they did, because the catalytic converter blew out on the way home.

If it wasn't one thing, it was another. On the night of the storm, they prayed that the Lord would see them through, which is what He did with the help of others.

Another time, Rose and Kayla went to the movies; both wore dresses. Outside there was freezing rain. All of a sudden, the car started to spit and sputter along the way. It finally came to a dead halt in the middle of the road. Rose said a little prayer, then told Kayla to pop the hood. Out of nowhere, a car filled with teenage guys stopped to ask them if they needed a ride somewhere. The girls gladly said yes. As they drove the girls home, they asked what was wrong with the car. Kayla told them that it was probably just out of gas. She gave them five dollars for the ride and said thanks.

The next morning, the girls found a note on their front door that the guys had used the five dollars for gas in the tank of the girl's car.

Kayla and Rose picked up the car, which started right up and ran fine ever since.

Just about the time that Rose was beginning to enjoy life, the walls came crashing in. Remember the girl who's father was an undercover cop, the girl who didn't make the cheerleading squad? He was still out for revenge. Rose was getting stopped for everything until she finally lost her license from having so many points racked up against her. She wasn't going to let this stop her. She traded her car in a for a sporty little Triumph instead.

First, she was granted a restricted driver's license to and from work. This was fine until her boss asked her to fill in for a girl at work. Rose needed the money, so she agreed. Rose was late for her curfew, but it only took five minutes to get home from where she worked. She hoped the cops would be too busy that night to be watching out for her.

Rose stopped to get some gas, when she saw two cop cars pull up in front and behind her. They read her the rights and hauled her off to jail in the middle of the night, a day before her twenty-seventh birthday!

Her bond was set for $250. Rose called Kayla and told her to come and get her. Kayla went around to the friends she knew who had money. Once she got what she needed, she went to rescue Rose. Rose was forever grateful that Kayla was her friend.

At her hearing, the court appointed a lawyer for her. She was sentenced to attend driving school and to do community service at the National Guards.

This didn't stop Rose from driving. She took on another job to help her with her expenses. At first, Jack didn't press charges for her to pay child support. Then he changed his mind.

Rose was in tears when she went to see the lawyer. He asked her if Jack ever abused her in any way. Rose told him the truth. Because there was a two-year statute of limitation, her lawyer was able to help her, but it cost four hundred dollars. Rose begged her parents for the money. This time, they helped her out even though they disagreed.

Rose didn't have to pay child support for two years. This made Jack furious. Whenever Rose and Jack agreed, Rose could see the girls for that length of time. This was written in their divorce decree. Jack would agree for the moment, but when Rose and Kayla arrived, he and the girls were gone.

This made Rose furious. He did this nearly every time Rose went to see the girls. She kept track of the occasions that he did this, and Kayla was her witness.

When it came time for Rose to pay child support again, Jack continued to play his games. Rose refused to pay until she got a court hearing. She was asked why she hadn't paid any child support for a year. She told the judge what was going on. The judge made her pay, but he also changed the visitation rights so that she could get the girls every other weekend. If Jack refused again, he'd get thrown in jail. Jack finally cooperated.

About every two months, Rose was thrown in jail for driving on a restricted license. She had to get around. Her friend couldn't take her because she was also working two jobs at the time. There were no buses available.

The next time she talked to her lawyer, he told her that somebody had her name on a dart board. He advised her to move out of state or get married.

Rose and Kayla had to go their separate ways because their electric bill kept getting higher and higher. And Kayla lost her night job, therefore, she couldn't pay her half of the rent anymore.

Kayla moved in with an old boyfriend, whereas Rose moved in with Margret across town in a posh town house.

They still kept in contact with each other. They knew their friendship would last forever.

9
Party Time

Rose began to live a wild and crazy lifestyle after she moved in with Margret. She hopped from bar to bar, hoping she'd meet Mr. Right. Instead, she found drugs and alcohol, a crutch to nurture her wounded soul.

Men clung to her like bees to a hive. Many one-night stands took place during this time. Rose had a high sex drive that just couldn't be quenched. This, too, is a symptom of manic depression.

She was now suffering from four symptoms, which drove her to the brink of insanity. They were: inappropriate irritability, inappropriate social behavior, insomnia, and high sex drive.

Because she was living on the high side of manic depression, she was able to deal with her problems. Whenever she dipped down into the depression side, she would take the drugs and drink to pull her up again. Her life was a yo-yo spinning on a tight string, just waiting to snap.

Her mother would call to tell her that she was sick and needed help, but Rose felt fine. She was sick of her mother's trying to run her life.

Rose didn't want to go to a doctor to take lithium, which she desperately needed. It had caused weight gain when she took it in the past. Rose ignored her mother's advice, continuing to drink and use drugs.

Rose was very fortunate that she never got hooked on her bad habits. She did get hooked on smoking cigarettes.

Rose was looking for a husband to settle down with, but all she found were one-night stands.

Then Rose met David. He liked to spend time with Rose. The two became inseparable. Rose thought for sure that this was a love that would last forever.

David took Rose to meet his parents. It was a two-hour trip, both ways. They took Rose's little Triumph. Rose didn't know a thing about cars, because her first husband was a mechanic and always took care of the cars.

On the way home, the Triumph kicked the bucket. It was a good thing they had been pulling into the driveway at home when this happened. The car had no oil to speak of, so the engine froze up.

When Rose brought it to the mechanic, they told her it would cost $900 to fix. Rose just didn't have the money.

She bought a beater car for a hundred instead. She not only lost her little sports car, but she never saw David again.

Rose and Margret had an agreement that they would leave each other's boyfriends alone. Rose didn't particularly care for Margret's boyfriends anyway.

One night, Margret was entertaining a boyfriend when Rose got home from work. They were introduced and Rose told Margret that she was going to bed downstairs. She changed into her pajamas and crawled into bed. She had just fallen asleep, when she was awakened by someone trying to crawl into bed with her. Rose was about to scream, when he covered her mouth with a kiss.

"The minute I saw you, I knew I wanted to be with you," he said.

"Get out of here right now!"

"Dennis, where are you?" called Margret.

"He's down here with me, Margret. Come get him, now!"

Margret blamed Rose for seducing him, which wasn't the case. Then she told Rose that she had two weeks to move.

Rose called Kayla, asking her if there was any room for her. Kayla had moved to a single-unit trailer in the same park that they had lived in before. She told Rose that she would find out if there was a single unit for Rose as well.

Rose lucked out. They had a unit for her for ninety dollars a month. It was a lot smaller than the one they shared in the beginning, but it would do for now.

Rose kept on partying at the bars, even though her father had told her that she would never find anyone decent in the bars. Rose was out to prove him wrong. Who needed parents, anyway? Rose didn't need anyone living her life for her, she was old enough to take care of herself.

Occasionally, Rose returned to the strip joint, where she met Jason. He was so handsome that it made Rose's skin crawl when he came near her. His voice sent chills up and down her spine.

He noticed Rose every time she came near. It was as if he had a magnet in his back pocket. He was so sexy.

One night, Rose was feeling sexy herself. She wore a black spandex mini dress, a white rabbit tailored jacket, stockings, a garter belt, with sexy lingerie underneath. She was hot, and Jason could feel the heat.

When it came time to slip him a dollar bill under his G-string, he slipped her the tongue, devouring her ruby red lips. He told her to wait for him after the show. Rose could hardly wait.

They arrived at his bachelor pad an hour later. Jason poured her a glass of peach schnapps, her favorite, while he danced for her in the living room. He was so romantic.

He slowly removed her garments, one piece at a time. She quivered from his touch. Rose never knew such passion and desire even existed.

Next, he took a silk sheet and spread it out on the living room floor. The glow of the candles, the scent of the incense, the taste of schnapps enhanced as Rose lay on the silk sheet, feeling his strong hands massaging her from head to toe.

Afterwards, he carried her to the bedroom, where they made passionate love for hours.

Rose went back to the strip joint, hoping to see Jason dance, but he had moved on. That's when she met Rick, another dancer. He needed a ride home one night, so Rose agreed to take him.

She was dressed in leather that night. Rick told her that he had to stop at a friend's house on the way home.

Rose stayed in the car while he went inside. Little did Rose know he had slipped a needle filled with heroin under the seat. He also had stashed some pot in her glove compartment.

Two cop cars surrounded her. They asked her what she was doing there. She told the officers that she was waiting for a friend. They told her to get out of the car, and they searched for drugs. When asked about the needle, Rose told them that she was diabetic, that the syringe was her insulin. They made her roll up her sleeves, looking for track marks. Rose had just gotten a blood test earlier that day. The cops asked her why she had one with her. Rose told them that she always kept one with her in case she needed it. She lied, but the cops believed her. They also questioned Rick when he got in the car.

After that, they left them alone. Rose chewed Rick out for hiding the drugs in her car. She dropped him off and went on her merry way.

A week went by without any signs of Jason. Rose thought she had lost him for good. At work, she moped around like she had lost her best friend.

One thing Rose learned about Jason was that if he didn't have anything important to say, he'd just as soon not talk at all.

In the middle of winter, the heater went out. Rose called Jason to see if she might be able to stay with him, but he had company coming, so she wasn't able to rely on him. He made sure of that.

Rose asked Captain Joe if she could stay with him until the heater was fixed. Captain Joe also lived in the trailer park. He was sixty-eight years old but was still a lively old fellow. He married a woman who was thirty-three, but it just didn't work out the way he had planned. She left him for a younger man.

Since Captain Joe was lonely, he offered Rose a place to stay while her trailer was being fixed. It ended up to be a week.

Winter and spring flew by without a word from Jason. Rose figured he had found someone else. She was a little disappointed, but managed to find someone else to replace him.

She met up with Dan and Fred, who were subcontractors for a major company there on business. They were both married.

Dan owned a private jet and a DeLorian. They surprised Rose one day when they picked her up to go shopping. She thought that was special. A couple of other gentlemen did the same for her. Rose was happy, but not satisfied. She wanted someone to love, someone to marry, someone special.

She was sick of the party scene, the one-night stands, the rounds of men that surrounded her. She wanted a husband, a home, and maybe a baby or two.

At first, she thought that Jason was the one for her, but he was unreliable from the beginning. Besides, he probably had a dozen women around his neck.

Rose and Kayla went to a bar one night to listen to the band. Rose spotted a man with light blonde hair and blue eyes. He was playing pool with his friend. After the two of them finished their game, they came over to the table to buy a round of drinks.

Introductions were made. Rose found out his name was Jeff. He was twenty-four and Rose was twenty-six at the time. There was something mysterious about Jeff. Rose thought he was handsome, but every now and then, she caught an evil glare in his eyes.

Jeff drove a sports car that he was very proud of. He asked Rose if she wanted to go for a ride. Rose agreed after she okayed it with Kayla.

Jeff drove like a maniac. He took Rose to the country and told her to get out of the car. Rose was spellbound. She obeyed his orders. He spun the car around and took off with lightning speed, leaving Rose in the trail of dust he left behind. Rose started walking in the dark, not knowing where she was at all. Just then, Jeff appeared in front of her, telling her to get back in the car. He was just joking around. Some joke. Rose didn't think it was too funny.

Jeff started coming to where Rose worked to see her. Whenever she talked to her male customers, Jeff would want to know all about it. He was very jealous. Rose thought he'd get over it, but he didn't. He'd get mad and walk out in a rage.

Rose moved in with Captain Joe for protection. Too many men were following her around, including Jeff. This way, Rose could go home to a nice secure environment. Not only that, but she didn't have to pay any rent. She was able to save a little bit of cash. She didn't have to strip anymore either. Her parents weren't too happy about her moving in with him, but Rose didn't care what they thought. She was a free woman, able to make her own choices. Why do parents have to be so smart?

The next thing Rose knew, Jeff was asking for her hand in marriage. She was shocked. Then she remembered her attorney's words, "either move out of state or get married."

This was the ticket Rose was looking for to clear her name. She knew what was bothering Jeff. First, he lost his brother to leukemia, then, a rack of steel car bumpers came off the line, where he worked, crushing his knee. No wonder why Jeff was impatient. He had too much time on his hands. Besides that, he was waiting for his settlement to come through any day or year.

Jeff was really a nice guy, except at times he acted strangely.

Rose invited Jeff to come over to meet Captain Joe. Jeff agreed, Captain Joe thought Jeff was a fine gentleman, so why did Rose keep having the feelings that there was something more wrong with Jeff than he was telling her?

Rose went to meet Jeff's parents for Sunday dinner. She liked his father, but his mother had that same funny way about her. Rose thought that it might just be her imagination.

She went ahead and agreed to marry Jeff on December 5, 1986. When Rose told Kayla the good news, she wasn't too happy. She thought Rose was making a huge mistake, but Rose refused to listen.

To make matters worse, Jason showed up a couple of days before the wedding to tell Rose that he loved her and that he missed her. Where had he been these last couple of months? What took him so long to realize that he loved her. Did he propose as well? No, he simply walked away without putting up a fight. Rose thought he was a coward and decided she was better off marrying Jeff than waiting for Jason to come around.

Rose was torn because she really loved Jason.

Finally, the big day came. Rose asked Kayla, who wasn't happy about it, to stand up for her. Rose also asked Mandy to be her maid of honor. Her husband, Pete, also stood up for them. They were married at the Hall of Justice.

After the vows were said, they headed back to their trailer for a small reception. Rose had borrowed her mother's blue dress for the special occasion.

They didn't take a honeymoon to some exotic place, only to Chicago to pick up some friends from the airport.

It turned out to be a nightmare for Rose. One she will always remember.

Rose kept her job at the local restaurant for a while, until she was caught stealing. Rose needed the money for bills, so she took it. This was poor judgment on Rose's part. Yes, poor judgment is also a symptom of manic depression.

She was fired on the spot. Mr. D wanted to know who else was doing this. Rose told him and said that she was sorry for taking money that didn't belong to her. She explained to Mr. D that she needed the money for bills.

He had no choice but to let her go.

Jeff didn't want Rose to work. But she had to find a job somewhere to pay her child support so that she wouldn't get thrown in jail.

Rose went to Jeff's appointment with his psychiatrist to figure out what was wrong with him. She found out that he was schizophrenic. He also was manic depressive. Two people with manic depression do not mix well together. Not at all!

When Rose found out the truth, she didn't know which way to turn. She was in a marriage that was doomed from the start.

No wonder Rose saw that something was strange about him. And yet, she couldn't put a finger on it.

Now that Rose was committed, how would she be able to get out of it? Jeff's psychiatrist told Rose if he ever got out of hand to let him know. She would need a restraining order to get him committed.

Rose was abused several times during the five-week marriage. She kept denying the truth about Jeff. She didn't want to be seen in public, for fear that someone might see her. Word got out to Kayla, who feared the worst would eventually happen. Either Jeff would kill Rose or vice versa.

One night Jeff and Rose went to a hockey game together in a town twenty miles away from home. On the way home from the arena, all hell broke loose. The roads were slippery. Rose kept trying to get out, hoping someone would see them and call the police. They came to B Avenue, where a cop was waiting.

Between holding Rose down and watching the road, Jeff went into a ditch. The cops took Rose back to the city, where she could be checked over, to make out a report for her. They also gave her a restraining order for her own safety. Then they called her parents to come and get her. Her father was not happy. It was 3:00 A.M. and the roads were bad.

Rose spent the night at her parents' house. In the morning, Jeff was calling, asking for Rose to forgive him. He wanted her to come back home. Rose knew the only way to have him committed to a mental institution was to call his psychiatrist and let him know what was going on, that Jeff had beaten her up on several occasions, threatening her with a knife and a gun as well.

Rose came back home to find Jeff crying, saying that he was sorry and that it would never happen again. Rose had a hard time believing him.

The next day, Jeff went to a friend's house. Rose stayed home to make her phone calls. She called the psychiatrist and told him about everything that was going on. He made arrangements with the cops, as well as with the mental hospital to make sure they would be ready for Jeff when he was brought in.

Rose stayed at Captain Joe's house when they brought him in. Once she knew she was safe, she packed up her belongings to keep at Captain Joe's house.

She changed the phone number because Jeff was calling every two minutes. She was afraid, so she called Jason. He agreed to letting her come over and spend the night. He treated her like a queen. She knew she couldn't stay with Jason, so when the morning came, she returned to Captain Joe's.

Rose and Jeff got an annulment. She kept the last name.

Rose enrolled in a writing class a couple of years after she left Jeff. Her instructors told her to write about something she knew first hand.

She wrote a fiction short story version titled "Deadly Desire." She sent it to a couple of magazines, but it was rejected as being unsuitable to those magazines.

"Deadly Desire" makes its debut in the next chapter.

10
Deadly Desire

Rose felt the warmth of the sun as its rays melted the first signs of winter. She noticed how beautiful the tiny snowflakes were as they glistened in the sunlight. The little diamonds from heaven formed a star-shaped cluster around the ring finger on her left hand. The significant symbol of love filled her eyes with a special sparkle.

As she entered the cozy family restaurant and bar, her best friend, Kayla, greeted her with a questioning look of concern.

"Where have you been? You knew we had to set up for a banquet."

"I'm sorry, Kayla, but ever since last night, I've—"

"No time for explanations, we've got to get busy."

Preparations went smoothly, and the one hundred place settings were ready and waiting just minutes before the guests arrived.

Just then, Rose couldn't remember if she had told Jeff to pick up her bridal bouquet and attendants' flowers from the florist or not.

Quickly, she turned, dashing towards the pay phones. Strawberries flew everywhere from one of the customers, wearing an off-white, chiffon dress, as they collided in the hallway. Rose noticed the cloud of smoke, while the lady furiously tried to wipe the strawberry margarita off her exquisite dress. Heads turned as she threw accusations with an air of disgust.

"You careless little wench! Your days will be cursed because of your stupidity. Rest assured, darling, I'll make sure you're fired."

"Thanks, but I quit!"

Rose trembled, as she fought back the tears of humiliation, experiencing the horror of the other ninety guests, who were falsely accusing her.

Aimlessly, her eyes darted through the crowded room as she sprinted towards the entrance, leaving a trail of tears behind her. Pushing through the glass doors, she felt the cool breeze against her crimson cheeks.

If only they could've given me my wedding day off. None of this would've ever happened, she thought.

It was just too much pressure coming from every direction at once. It certainly didn't help matters any knowing Jeff the way he was.

Just six months earlier, he had the accident at work where a rack of steel, chrome-plated car bumpers had fallen off the line and crushed his knee completely out of socket.

Bills kept piling up, with no relief in sight. It seemed as though the pressure inside Jeff continuously mounted, causing him to lash out periodically.

It was like living with a caged tiger. If he couldn't have his freedom, he'd attack whoever he could.

During the two years previous to his injury, Jeff was calm, fun to be with, loving, athletic, and carefree.

Could it be that he was suffering from a Dr. Jekyll–Mr. Hyde personality complex?

As she entered their mobile home, that train of thought momentarily left her.

On the kitchen table stood a milky white vase holding a long-stemmed rose in all its beauty, capturing a ray of sunlight coming through the window. The little note propped next to the vase, added just the right touch:

> I love you, sweetheart! May this day, forever, be a promise of the love we cherish, as we share our lives together.
> With all my heart,
> Jeff

Her worries had been for nothing, she thought, as she carefully opened the box to gaze at the delicate bouquet of a corsage.

As tradition has its place, her grandmother had embroidered "Love" onto a white, lace handkerchief, which would be solemnly placed around the handle of her bridal bouquet. Rose said a prayer as she wrapped the tiny lace hanky around the handle.

With the clock ticking the minutes away, she started making the final arrangements necessary to make it to the justice of peace on time.

An aura of deception gave presence to the small, empty courtroom, upon her arrival. The last time Rose set foot inside those chambers, her first husband received custody of her daughters, through a devious plan of action. This time, however, Rose felt that by marrying Jeff she could eventually get her daughters back. Maybe her intentions were wrong, but she felt it was the only thread of hope left to hang onto.

Vows were exchanged as their token of love was witnessed by the few friends gathered with them.

As for Rose, the expectations she had been longing for would at last be reality. Walking hand in hand down the aisle with Jeff secured her dreams for a bright and promising future.

Their honeymoon suite awaited their arrival in Chicago. Traffic had been unbearable as they tried to make it to the airport on time.

Close friends of Jeff and Rose had just flown in from California, waiting to take part in this blessed event.

Celebration of the gala affair took place with a festive dinner. Bottles of champagne were presented for the toast, and soft, romantic music serenaded from the background.

Jeff and Rose had been under the impression that their friends needed a ride from the airport back to Grand Rapids. However, the arrangements for dinner, limousine service, and a bridal suite, was part of a surprise wedding gift.

As Rose glanced at Jeff in the back of the limousine, she noticed an edginess about him.

"Rose, are you still working at Brann's as a waitress?" innocently probed her friend from California.

"To be honest, after today, I'm not really sure."

"What do you mean by that?" questioned Jeff.

"I sort of walked out during lunch."

"You *what*?" he asked, as if he couldn't believe what he was hearing.

"I'm sorry, babe, but the pressure was too much," she replied with a tremble in her voice.

"Excuse me. Driver, I'd like to pull over, please."

"Jeff, what are you doing?"

"I want you out of this car and out of my life, *now!*"

Instantly, he grabbed her with a deathly grip, and with a shove, she was out the door.

As the limo pulled out of sight, Rose lay crippled on the sidewalk, pain enveloping her. Gradually, she found her legs able to move. She picked out the pieces of gravel from her kneecaps and rose slowly to her feet.

She shook her head, trying to clear the cobwebs. Did this actually happen, or was her imagination playing tricks on her?

The tears fell softly, blurring her vision, as she walked along the main street. A light from a tiny gas station was the only warmth she felt on this cold December night.

Perhaps a cup of coffee would help decide what her next step should be. As she looked outside the window from the small cafe table, a silver, sporty, Chrysler pulled up to the pump. She couldn't believe who she saw getting out of the car, making his way to the door.

"Can we talk, Rose?" asked Jeff, with a sheepish look. His puppy-dog eyes melted her heart.

"I suppose," she half-heartedly replied.

"I'm sorry, sweetheart. I don't know what possessed me to act in such an irrational way. Please forgive me."

His words were so soothing, as he brushed away her tears and gently lifted her chin to gaze into her swollen eyes.

"Honey, I love you. Please come home with me."

It was an offer she couldn't refuse. After all, how else was she supposed to get back to Grand Rapids at 1:00 A.M.? Besides, how could she hold anything against him, knowing the pressure he had been under?

He kissed her tender lips promising never to hurt her again. Gradually, she rose from her seat, taking his arm securely, as they walked back to the car. If only she had considered this incident to be a warning, her future could've been a lot brighter. Instead, she fell victim to his deception.

The drive back from Chicago to Grand Rapids, seemed to be an eternity. Her eyelids, felt like slabs of granite, as she desperately strained to keep them open.

Her mind was exhausted from the long emotional day. Reluctantly, she fell asleep, resting at last, peacefully. It was as though the Lord granted her the serenity to restore the strength she needed to carry on.

Rose awoke to the aroma of coffee brewing in the kitchen. Sipping her morning cup of coffee, she watched the birds gleefully chirping, as a soft ray of sunlight danced across the window.

"Good morning, sunshine. Breakfast is ready when you are. Just relax, let me serve you with a smile." He reached over to hug her.

It baffled Rose to think that Jeff could be such a gentleman and yet without a second's warning could erupt like a raging volcano. What had caused his explosion? Would it happen again?

Finished with breakfast, Rose got dressed, preparing herself for the household chores.

Contemporary religious music set the scenario as she began to busy herself with a mop and bucket. Somehow, the music enlightened her soul. Maybe this change of pace could rejuvenate her in some way.

Actually, it was just what the doctor ordered. Her spirits lifted during the week. Jeff had calmed down and displayed his overwhelming passion by supporting her in every way possible. He helped her around the house, attempted to serenade her, and prepared romantic candlelight dinners, trying to make his way back into her heart.

By the end of the week, Rose felt strong enough to search for a new job. At last, she found hope when a company she had applied at called to set up an interview.

"Honey, I have an interview, tomorrow at 9:00 A.M. for the factory job I told you about."

"Congratulations, sweetheart, I knew you could do it." Jeff looked pleased.

With anticipation, Rose pressed her blouse, checked her skirt and blazer, polished her matching shoes, making sure everything gave her a professional appearance. After all checks had balanced she was ready for her debut in the morning. She then set the alarm to go off prompt at 7:30 A.M.

The ringing in her ears made her jump out of bed, not noticing that Jeff had already started his day.

The warm shower was somewhat relaxing to her tense body. Preparations went smooth, considering she was ready to go within an hour.

Where was Jeff? Did he run to the store to buy a pack of cigarettes? Time was running out and still no sign of him, 8:45 A.M. Where was he?

Jeff had taken the car. Reluctantly, Rose called to cancel her interview. She made the excuse that she had car trouble and hoped that they would reschedule her interview for a later date. Perhaps Jeff was trying to tell her something, but why today, knowing how important that job was? She just couldn't understand.

She changed into her blue jeans, turned on the radio, and started a batch of laundry. She knew Jeff would eventually return with an explanation.

The day dragged on; still no sign of Jeff. Rather than mope around the house, since the chores were done, she concentrated on dinner. Maybe, a nice home-cooked meal would ease her anger. While she peeled potatoes, the phone rang.

"Hello."

"Hi, sweetheart. How did the interview go?"

"That's a stupid question. Where did you take off to?"

"I'm in Detroit."

"Whatever possessed you to go there? You knew I needed the car this morning." Rose said, with a note of sarcasm in her voice.

"I'm sorry, honey, but I forgot that I promised to give Rod a ride. We had to take care of a little business this morning."

"Why don't you start thinking about your wife for a change?"

"That's why I'm calling you now."

"Don't you think it's a little bit late, Jeff? You could've left me a note this morning."

"Let's not argue, babe, I'll be home in two hours. I love you."

Rose slammed down the receiver. She was furious. The nerve he had, calling her at the end of the day to apologize. There was no excuse for his selfish actions. It was time for her to put a halt to his childish behavior. She walked down the hallway toward the bedroom. In rage and desperation, she grabbed her suitcases, opened the closet, and threw her clothes in a heap on the bed. Perhaps her actions would speak louder than words this time.

"Mom," she cried from one end of the phone, "I'm coming home. Jeff and I got into a fight. I can't take it anymore."

"Rose, what's wrong?" her mother asked, concern in her voice.

"I don't want to talk about it right now. I just want to come home. I'll see you in a couple of hours."

So much for the myth, "lived happily ever after." Cinderella didn't have problems like this; why should she? Determined to teach Jeff a lesson, she continued to pack her suitcases with her personal belongings until she had gathered everything. So that Jeff wouldn't suspect anything when he got home, she hid them in the spare bedroom, which was used for storage.

She heard the front door open. Her heart began to beat like a war drum pounding the rhythm of terror. Rose walked down the hallway. She noticed that Jeff took his shoes off but left his coat on. There was a moment of silence as their eyes met.

"Hi, sweetheart; what's for dinner?" asked Jeff casually, as if nothing were wrong.

"I don't know. Why don't you ask Rod?" she replied, as he tried to kiss her on the cheek.

"I'm sorry, Jeff; you'll have to make your own dinner." she replied, as she brushed past him to grab her coat from the couch.

He shook her by the shoulders, turning her abruptly to face him.

"Where do you think you're going?"

"I need some time to think things over. Let go of me!"

Pushing past him, she made her way toward the spare bedroom. He followed close behind, trying to convince her not to leave.

"I won't let you go, Rose. You're my wife and you belong here with me."

Ignoring him, she entered the spare room, grabbed her suitcases, and turned toward the door. Petrified, she looked up, to see Jeff standing in front of the entrance. Briefly, an illusion of James Bond coming to her rescue with a hand revolver concealed behind his coat, vanished. She heard a click from the gun that he held.

"I love you Rose! If you leave, I'll kill myself."

"Please, Jeff, put the gun down."

Beads of sweat trickled down the back of her neck as she tried to persuade her husband not to kill himself.

"I love you, dear. Please don't take your life," she pleaded.

"I'm warning you for the last time. If you walk out that door, I'll pull the trigger."

"If you put the gun down, I promise I won't leave you."

Rose put her suitcases down on the floor to reassure Jeff that she would stay. Gently, he laid the gun down to rest.

She wrapped her arms around him, resting her head upon his chest, and the teardrops fell like rain. Silently, they held on to each other. Knowing in their hearts that the vows they made for life gave serenity to the chaos they felt around them.

At times, Rose just wanted to run back home, to be under the protection of her parents. There, at least, she felt safe. Yet, at twenty-six, she knew that she was considered to be an adult. It was time to start living her own life.

Could it be that Jeff was actually suffering from the psychological disorder, schizophrenia? Impossible. Jeff appeared to be normal in every way. He just had a bad temper. Not knowing how to control it was his problem.

No use trying to find a job. It was time to start building a home together. Rather than fighting, trying to tear down the walls, using reverse psychology might be the key desperately needed. They decided that teamwork would be the best policy. After all, Jeff's workman's compensation check could pay the bills. It would be tight, but in time, things were bound to get better.

The interest they chose together was hockey. Jeff was a devoted fan. Actually, Rose didn't really care for the sport that much until Jeff explained the theory behind it. Then she started taking an interest in it. Together they watched the game on TV. The next thing she knew, Jeff was asking her to go with him to one of the games. Right away, Rose questioned about the cost. She knew that ten dollars might have to last them for a week. They really couldn't afford it if both of them went. She knew how important it was for Jeff to get away. Showing her sincerity, she surrendered, allowing Jeff to go alone. Little did she know Rod, Jeff's friend, had gotten them the tickets ahead of time. Jeff never said a word and left without her.

Alone at last. As soon as he left, Rose started on a project she had been thinking about for the past three weeks. It was a hand-quilted pillow for the couch.

Patiently, she stitched the delicate design. If she worked at it, she would have it finished by the time Jeff got home.

Time flew by while she stuffed the pillow, stitching the sides together. She couldn't believe that four hours had already passed. Jeff would be home in an hour, which gave her just enough time to bathe, slip into a sexy, lace teddy, and sip on a glass of peach schnapps on the rocks before he arrived.

When Jeff walked in the front door, he noticed the candle burning on the kitchen table. The little note attached read: "I have a surprise for you in the bedroom."

Quietly, he slipped into the room. Rose had drifted off to sleep. A kiss on the forehead awoke the sleeping beauty. Gently, he caressed her neck, making his way to her luscious lips. Most definitely, a vision of beauty.

As he passionately kissed her, Jeff noticed the taste of alcohol on her breath.

"Who have you been sleeping with, you drunken whore?"

"Nobody, I've been waiting for you."

"Get out of my bed!"

He yanked her to her feet and grabbed her by the throat. Squeezing the breath from her terrified body, he furiously yelled.

"You slut! I want you out of my life, *now!*"

His hands let go for a brief second as he reached for his cigarette, which was burning in the ashtray next to the bed.

Gasping for air, Rose felt his fingers as he clenched a fistful of her golden locks of hair.

Pain shot through the back of her neck, as she felt the hot ashes sizzle her flesh. Turning, Jeff grabbed her nightie, tearing it to shreds.

"I hate it, Jeff!"

She tried to reach the door, crawling on her hands and knees. She reached up and grabbed ahold of the doorknob and opened the door. Jeff slammed it against her head, hitting her in the eye. She bit him in the leg. He struck her with a powerful blow to the head with his foot, followed by a shove, which sent her sprawling through the door, to the frozen ground below.

She scrambled to her feet. No time to waste, she thought, racing next door to her girlfriend's house. Thank goodness, she was home.

Kayla appeared shocked when she opened the door and found Rose, half naked, battered, trembling with fear. Kayla gave her a blanket to keep her from shaking and called the police.

Within minutes, the officers arrived to investigate the case. Rose fought back her tears as she explained in detail what had happened. With a sympathetic ear, they patiently listened to her story, then carefully checked out the bruises and burns that covered her body.

"Ma'am, now that you're safe, there's really nothing we can do. I suggest that you go down to the courthouse first thing Monday morning to press charges." And with that statement, they left.

"So, this is what you call police protection," remarked Kayla, with a snide tone of voice. "I don't believe this nonsense! Don't worry, Rose; I'll make sure the cops are informed when you go home to get your belongings. As for now, you need to get some sleep."

Kayla grabbed a pillow and blanket from her bed, then set up the studio couch in the living room. She handed Rose one of her night shirts and gave her a hug.

"Rose, you'll be safe here. I'll make sure of that."

Exhausted, Rose crawled into bed. Her head was pounding with every second the alarm clock ticked away. Her body felt like a punching bag after a prize fighter took out his frustrations on it.

Eventually, she drifted off to sleep, her body continued to flinch as she tossed and turned throughout the night.

She woke up with her head still ringing. As she opened her eyes, she saw Kayla answer the phone.

"Just a minute, Jeff, I'll see if she is awake."

Terrified, she answered the phone.

"Honey, I'm sorry, please come home. I can't live without you."

"Jeff, I'd like to go to church first. I'll talk to you when I come to get my clothes."

As Rose hung up the receiver, Kayla confronted her, reassuring their friendship.

"Don't worry, Rose, I'll notify the cops just before you get back. Just ask the Lord for protection. You can wear one of my dresses and use my car if you'd like."

Rose got dressed and was ready to leave within minutes. Bravely, she drove to church, knowing that the Lord would protect her from danger.

Faithfully, she listened to the sermon about strength coming from above. As she asked the Lord to grant her the strength and courage she needed, Jeff kept himself busy around the house.

Casually resting on the arm of the over-stuffed living room chair, he plotted his deadly attack.

The icy cold ointment gradually formed beads of sweat as he penetrated the lotion into his fiery palms. Such a soothing effect.

The black leather gloves secretly hid the imprint of his identification, leaving only the weapons as an indication of his deadly desire to extinguish their precious love.

Concealed behind the family portrait lay the butcher knife waiting to carve out her heart.

Beneath the hand-quilted pillow she had patiently sewn out of love nestled an iron horseshoe wrapped with her lace handkerchief. The same one, just five weeks before, had been solemnly wrapped around her bridal bouquet, promising their love forever.

The jealousy raging within kept pounding the rhythm in vain: *I love you so, my sweetest Rose, please my love, please don't go.*

Sitting alone in the back of a small nondenominational church, Rose, in a terrifying grip of fear, uttered a trembling prayer for help.

"Father, I humbly come before you. Please, God, don't let him kill me."

Gradually, she brought the car to a halt in front of the house. She walked up to the front door and knocked, waiting for Jeff to let her in. As he opened the door, Rose noticed the black leather gloves he wore.

That's odd, she thought. *Why is he wearing gloves and beating his fists together?*

Just then, he thrust the iron horseshoe in her ribs. The pain was excruciating and caused her to double over, clenching her side as she fell to the ground.

"Oh God, please!"

Faintly, she could hear the sirens getting closer and closer. At last, help was on its way.

Through the corner of her eye she saw the blade glisten in the sunlight, just moments away from carving out her heart.

Her eyes flashed open as she sat up in bed. She tried to catch her breath as she listened to the ambulance sirens pass by her bedroom window.

11
Bluegrass Fever

It was the summer following Rose's annulment with Jeff. Rose joined a pen-pal club, which matched her up with Julie, who lived in Indiana. Julie invited Rose to go to a Bluegrass festival for a weekend with her at Green Acres in Indiana. Julie was a big fan of the Ramblers.

Rose had never been to a festival before. This was something new and exciting.

When they arrived at the park, there were tents and campers parked everywhere. Rose waited to unpack her tent, because the Ramblers were on stage when they arrived. Rose took one look at the band and knew why Julie was excited. Julie thought that Andy was the greatest, but Rose had her heart set on Travis.

Rose grabbed her spoons, then headed for a tree near the stage to lean against. Just as soon as the band left the stage, a man yelled at Rose to move away from the tree as quickly as possible. There, just above where Rose was standing, was a huge, black water moccasin curled around the trunk of the tree, waiting for his chance to bite Rose. The man quickly removed the snake from the tree, killing it with a single blow to the head. So close to death was Rose, that it sent shivers up and down her spine.

After that, Rose played her spoons from her lawn chair. Several artists played fiddles, banjos, guitars, et cetera. They had traveled many miles to perform at this festival.

Rose and Julie met up with Brenda. The three of them hung around together for the entire weekend.

Sunday was a beautiful sunny day. Rose took out her Bible and began to meditate. She asked the Lord to show her a sign. She wanted to find someone who knew how to help her, to give her some insight as to what was up the road aways. What would her future be like? Would she ever remarry? Have any more children?

She needed some direction. While she was thumbing through her Bible, she kept running into the word, "Love." Surely, this was the key. But where would she find the person who held the key?

After she finished, she met up with Julie and Brenda. They wanted to go check out the record stands, so Rose went along.

They ended up near an old Indian who sat behind the record table. He watched them very carefully. Then he spoke.

He spoke to Brenda first.

"Pretty lady, you have eyes for my son." (She is now married to his son!)

Then, he spoke to Julie.

"Pretty eyes of blue, many doors will be opened unto you." (She now works for the Old Opry Hotel as a secretary!)

"And as for you, pretty Rose, I want to talk to you."

She went over and sat next to him. He asked her a question.

"What are these lonely people looking for? What are they missing in their lives? Don't answer me right now; just watch."

Rose knew the answer but kept silent. Then she saw him pull out his wallet. On the back of it, he wrote, "Love."

Rose was amazed. Next, he read her palm. He knew she had two children, two marriages, both to abusers. He told Rose that as soon as the storm clouds rolled away, she would have happiness forever.

Rose thanked the Lord for answering her prayer. This was the first time Rose had her prayers answered so quickly.

That day, Travis helped Rose pack her car, and kissed her good-bye.

Rose left for the long journey home. When Rose got back to Captain Joe's house, she packed up her belongings and moved back home for awhile.

Later, she found out from Julie that a girl with a unicorn tattoo had been killed by the lake at the Bluegrass festival. Julie was worried because Rose also had a unicorn tattoo.

Two years later, Rose had the chance to see another Bluegrass festival. This one was in Michigan. Rose went with her boyfriend, Dave, this time. Julie had to work, so she couldn't go. The Ramblers didn't make their appearance at this one. A band from Ireland did. They were fantastic. The weather was beautiful.

Rose played her spoons to the beat of the bagpipes. When Sunday rolled around, Rose headed for a grove of pines to meditate. She asked the Lord to come to earth to see and hear the wonderful music. It was a grandiose notion, but Rose believed that all things were possible. So, she didn't think anything was wrong by asking the Lord to come to earth to experience this beautiful day.

Rose sat by a pine tree, smoking a cigarette while she glanced around. About fifty feet away from her, a small group in white robes gathered around. There was a man in the middle with a beard, mustache, and shoulder-length hair, giving the other twelve something to eat and drink. Then he kissed them on the cheek and gave them a hug before they returned to the group.

Rose saw a couple walking down the pathway through the pines. She asked them what that group was. They told her that it was a holy mass. She asked if she could join them, but they told her that no one was allowed to join.

Rose tried to sneak closer to get a better look. When she did, the group disappeared, vanished into thin air.

Rose couldn't believe her eyes. Things like this just don't happen every day. Rose kept this vision for a long time, never saying a word to anybody, not even to Dave.

12
Truckin' U.S.A.

Rose moved in with her parents, but she felt very uncomfortable because of the flashbacks that she had of her father.

She had to find a way out of there as soon as possible. They treated her as if she were still eighteen.

Rose was twenty-seven, old enough to make her own decisions.

She went to a temporary job service to find a place to work close by. She started working at the same place her mother did. They both worked for an office furniture factory.

At first, Rose stayed by herself during lunch, reading a book to keep her mind occupied.

One night, a man by the name of Eric came over and sat by her. They worked in the same station together. Eric had strawberry-blonde hair, a beard, and mustache. Rose thought he was very handsome.

He started complaining about his wife. Rose could see how torn up he was. If only she could help him, she thought. Eric was a deacon at the church he attended and a father of two small children, whom he loved dearly, but he couldn't live with his wife any longer.

One night after work, he took Rose to a park. There they had a long discussion about where he could go to get away for awhile. He told Rose that he used to be a trucker. That's it! They would travel together in the big rig. Rose needed to get away as much as Eric did.

Rose was also working as a sales rep for a carpet cleaning business. One day, Eric showed up. Rose was shocked, but she was also pleased.

"I found a truckin' job today. They want me to start as soon as possible. I need a place to stay tonight, because tomorrow I leave for New York. Will you go with me, Rose, please?"

"Oh, yes, Eric! I will go with you."

"Tell your boss that you quit."

That's exactly what Rose did.

Every night that Rose worked at the factory, her mother would call, just to check up on her. This made the foreman a little edgy until finally he fired Rose just before she left for New York.

Rose didn't tell her parents a thing. She spent the night with Eric, and left the next morning at 8:00 A.M.

They spotted Rose's car in a shopping plaza parking lot at the other end of town.

Rose hopped in the rig, feeling like queen of the highway. This was great. Rose never rode in a semi before. It was fall, the colors were beautiful.

They traveled to New York, to Pennsylvania, then to Georgia, to Florida, and on to Texas, then back home. This went on for months. They even had a layover in Florida for the Christmas vacation.

Each time they came back, they stayed with Sam, a friend of Rose's. Sam didn't seem to mind at all. There was one trip that Rose couldn't go with Eric, so she stayed home with Sam. While she was taking a shower, Sam thought that he'd join her. Rose never gave him an invitation; he just got in the shower with her. Rose quickly got out and got dressed. She told Sam that if he ever tried that stunt again, she'd tell Eric about it.

When Eric got back, he told Rose that he'd be making one last trip to Florida. Rose went along for the ride. She had to get away from Sam. She told Eric all about it. They decided to get an apartment together in Michigan. Rose didn't have any money, so when she got back, she'd have to talk to her parents.

Eric told Rose that he wouldn't be able to move in with her because he was thinking about going back home for awhile.

When Rose returned home, she went to her parents' house. They asked her where she had been. She told them that she had been truckin' with a friend. Her parents were upset with her, but they gave her the money anyway.

Rose headed out to see Kayla, who was now living with her boyfriend, Kurt. She bought a bottle of peach schnapps for the trip. It was gone by the time she reached Saugetuck.

When Rose reached Kayla's apartment, her eyes were swollen and red from crying over Eric. She loved him dearly. But it wasn't meant to be.

Rose remembered a conversation that Kayla, Kurt, and she had about Kayla getting pregnant. Kayla wanted a baby so bad, but Kurt had had an operation, so he couldn't have any more children.

Rose prayed for a miracle for Kayla, that she would get pregnant by Kurt. Sure enough, in October of that year, Kayla found out she was pregnant.

During the holiday season, Kayla had plenty of drinks for company when they stopped over, but she had none for herself.

Rose drank a couple of glasses of wine when she arrived. Sue, a friend of Kayla's needed a ride to her car. Rose offered to take her, even though she still didn't have her driver's license back.

After dropping Sue off, Rose headed for Kayla's apartment. Only she never made it back until four hours later. A cop car was waiting right around the corner. They stopped Rose because they said that she didn't make a complete stop at the corner, which she did.

They gave her a breathalizer test, which Rose passed because she breathed ever so slightly that it wouldn't register. She told the cops that she had asthma. They believed her, but they still took her in for a suspended driver's license.

When Rose arrived at the jailhouse, they wanted to stick her in the drunk tank with twenty men. Rose told the cops that she had enough money for bail. With that, they released her.

As soon as Rose was released, she stuck her thumb out to hitch a ride back to Kayla's apartment. She was lucky. A driver just happened to be going her way.

Kayla was surprised to see Rose at five in the morning. She thought for sure that after Rose dropped Sue off, she had headed for home. But that wasn't the case at all.

Kurt asked Rose where her car was. She told him that they had impounded her car. Good thing Rose had all that money with her.

Kurt found out where the car was. Rose couldn't get it herself because she didn't have a license. Kurt had to drive her to the outskirts of town, because they were escorted by a cop.

Eric called Rose at her parents' house to see how she was doing. He also called to see if Rose wanted to make one last trip with him.

Rose called her lawyer to let him know what had happened. He told her to enjoy her trip. He said it would give him enough time to bargain with the judge over her case.

Rose packed her bags and headed for Texas with Eric. They arrived in Florida to pick up a load first, then headed to Texas.

They had a wonderful trip. Eric gave Rose enough money to get the apartment when they got back. He told Rose that he was sorry, he couldn't stay. He had to go back home where he belonged.

Rose moved into an apartment complex close to the city. She found a job as a switchboard operator for one of the finest hotels in town within walking distance from her apartment.

Saying good-bye to Eric was the hardest thing for her to do. Rose felt lost without him. She thought she would never fall in love again. But as time went on, destiny would prove her wrong.

13
Onward Bound

When Rose moved into her apartment, she had very little to move. Once all the furniture was in the place still looked bare. Rose was pleased with the way it looked. Modern poverty at its finest.

The alarm clock failed to go off because of a power shortage during the night. Rose hustled around the apartment, trying to be on time to catch the bus going into town. She ran out the entrance to her building, when she saw the bus whiz by. Now she would be an hour late because of the bus schedule.

As she was waiting for the bus, a black man, Darrel, walked past her. He said, "hi" in a friendly tone.

Rose was a little shy at first because of the rape in the past. But she got up enough courage to talk to him while he was scraping the snow off his car. She asked him if there was any chance that he would be traveling her way. As a matter of fact, he was. He offered to give her a ride. Rose gracefully accepted. After that day, they became the best of friends.

That night, Darrel stopped by to share a cup of coffee. He noticed how bare her apartment was. It just so happened that he had ordered new furniture and didn't know what to do with the old. So he offered it to Rose. The next thing she knew, they were carrying the old furniture to her apartment. Rose thanked him for his kindness. She was touched.

The next day, Rose found an old hope chest out by the dumpster. She hauled it back to her room. She now had her apartment completely furnished.

Soon after Rose met Darrel, she met Marie, who lived across the hall from her. They became good friends.

Marie was white, but her boyfriend was black. Marie was in love, but her parents disowned her because of her love for a black guy. Her parents were prejudiced. Rose's parents were prejudiced also. Rose knew that if that ever happened to her, she would be disowned as well.

Rose came from a different generation, where all were created equal. There was good and bad in both races.

Rose had dated a few black men, who treated her with respect, but her mother became very upset by this. Rose didn't care as long as she was happy.

She remembered one time when Tom Sheen went with her to pick up her girls, her ex had a fit. But he let the girls go. Tom took them to the movies where he worked. The four of them had a great time.

Her mother got wind of it. She told Rose that if she dated another black guy, she would be disowned.

From that point on, Rose kept her private life a secret. What mother doesn't know won't hurt her.

The time that Rose spent alone gave her a creative edge. Rose asked her parents for the old typewriter they had at home. Her father brought it to her. Rose was very excited, but her father was very upset with her new found creative will.

"I don't know why you want this thing," he grumbled.

"Because I want to write a book."

"That's a stupid idea, Rose! Do you know how hard it is to write one? You just don't have what it takes."

Rose knew that her father was discouraging her because he was afraid of what she would write about. She was bound and determined to write a book about her life. She had made a commitment with the Lord when she was thirteen to write a book, even though at the time, she wasn't sure what the book would be about.

Her father left, and Rose began to type. She saw an ad in a magazine for poetry. It was a poetry contest. No experience necessary.

Rose also received information about a writing school for short stories and novels. Besides that, a place where your poetry could be used as lyrics for a song.

She felt that if the Lord didn't want her to write, that she wouldn't have received all this information. It was like a sign from heaven.

Little did Rose know that writing is also good therapy for someone suffering with a mental illness. It helps the victim recover. Rose found out that she was able to put the pieces of her life together like one big jigsaw puzzle.

A Teardrop of Love

If
the
weatherman
promised sunshine,
whenever, it would rain,
would you patiently keep waiting
while your teardrops fell against the pane?
To simply sit and wonder how different
life might have been, if only you
would've stayed with the one
who poured out sunshine
from within.

Hope for Tomorrow

Hope is the faith
it takes to believe
in yourself.
Only *you* can brighten your future
If today seems
depressing,
start tomorrow with
the hope of it
becoming a better day.
To walk solemnly with
your chin toward
the ground
overlooks the beautiful
sunshine around you.
Cast your shadows behind
to let the hope
you believe in,
shed light upon
the pathway of happiness,
for beyond the horizon,
leads the road to success.

Reflections of You

To have met face to face,
silently passing by on the street,
would simply be a whisper in the wind.
as though the sunshine
enlightens the heart.
The silence of darkness
casts a shadow upon life's pathway.
To acknowledge a friend
from the past or the present
shows a reflection of you.

When times are good,
friends are present.
When times are bad,
a friend is desperately needed.
It's sad, but true.
Friendships are meant to be cherished.
Just remember,
no matter, what you do,
others see,
a reflection of you.

The Life of a Rose

Love is a rose
born sweet as honey,
attracting with its subtle scent.
Growing amongst thorn and good ground,
wanting to be as all the rest.
Yielding quiet beauty,
rainbow of color
sure seed forever.
One could learn from you.
Creation of God,
soft pedal feelings,
growing wild throughout the vines.
Harmless creature trusting nature.
A part of the universe
living life allowed thee.
Death is dark, awaiting in the shadow
of one so meek and true.
The innocence of her beauty forever
remains to be seen as:
The life of a Rose.

Rose entered the poetry in four different contests, which were sponsored by the National Library of Poetry, the Poetry Center, the National Poetry Anthology, and the American Poetry Anthology.

Every one of her poems was published, including "The Life of a Rose," which was written by Kayla and Rose together.

Nineteen eighty-eight was a good year for Rose. Her mother praised her, but her father disgraced her.

"Did you get paid for this?" he asked.

"No, but I got published." Rose replied proudly.

Her father just wanted her to quit writing because he knew that if Rose would ever write a book, she would tell his secret that he hid from her mother all these years.

Rose knew she was on the right track when "Reflections of You" became a hit single in the music world.

She went on to write, "Deadly Desire" for her short-story class. Rose was on a roll. She had always wanted to be a writer.

It made her feel good about herself once again. She knew she was on the right track.

One day while she was working at the hotel, a man from Chicago introduced himself. Rose knew she wasn't supposed to fraternize with the public, but this man was offering a free trip to Chicago and back for Rose. How could she pass up an opportunity of a lifetime? She couldn't. She gave him her home phone, and away she went. She got fired for it, but she didn't care. She could always find another job.

When Dan heard that she lost her job, he told her to put in an application at the train station as a service attendant. Rose had never heard about the trains going cross-country before. Dan told her all about it. She had been a waitress before, but never on a train. Besides, this would give her a chance to see the country.

When Dan met Rose at the train station, they stopped in the personnel office, where Rose applied for the job. They told her that they would be hiring in the spring.

Rose fell in love with Chicago. Everything was new and exciting. It was such a big city.

Rose took a big chance by accepting the invitation from Dan. That was poor judgment on Rose's part, but poor judgment is a symptom of manic depression.

Dan turned out to be a gentleman, so Rose's worries turned to happiness. She had a great time.

On the train back home, Rose met another gentleman from Chicago, Bart, a producer in Chicago. He also invited Rose back to Chicago. She could hardly wait until she went again.

When Rose got home from her trip, reality set in. She had no job Neither did she have money to pay the rent.

She was depressed, but something gave her the power to move on. She went to the welfare office to see if they could help. They told her they could give her emergency funding for her rent, this time only, if she would go to classes during the day.

Rose went to the classes about finding a job. When she came home from school, she decided to go job hunting. She went inside a cozy little bar, applying for a waitress job. The bartender told her that they weren't accepting any applications at the moment, so Rose moved on. She went to a wholesale jewelry outlet.

It just so happened they were hiring. Rose got the job.

She couldn't walk to the job, because it was too far. Tom Sheen came to her rescue once again. He was a musician. For some reason, Rose was meeting all the right people when she needed them.

Rose was a secretary, having full access to the copying machine. One of the girls in the office knew what she was doing. Somehow, word got out. Rose lost her job again.

Rose took the train to Chicago to meet Bart. She also checked on her application, but nothing was going on there.

On her trip home, Rose noticed a guy who looked very familiar to her, but she couldn't place him. So she asked him where he worked; then both remembered where they knew each other from. It was the cozy little bar where Rose applied for a job.

Rose told him about her writing career, which interested him. As they continued to get to know each other, Glen introduced himself. Rose asked him if he could give her a ride home from the train station and he took her home.

Once inside her apartment, Glen felt at ease. Rose offered him a cup of coffee. He stayed and listened to the soft music playing in the background while he read her poetry. He was impressed.

Before he left, he kissed her passionately. "Good night, Rose," he said.

During the next month, Rose saw Glen every day. They were inseparable. Rose knew the trouble she would be in if she didn't find a job soon, so she clung onto Glen with all her might.

She finally got up enough courage to tell Glen that she was getting kicked out of her apartment and had no place to go.

Glen felt sorry for her, so the next thing he knew, she was moving in.

Rose was going to move a roommate in, but it would have become too crowded. Besides, Rose wanted to try writing a book. When Rose wrote, she listened to her soft music, lit a candle, burned incense, and meditated back to her past. If her concentration was disturbed, she couldn't write.

With her working days and Glen working nights, it was perfect for her. Until she came down with writer's block.

She found a daytime job as a secretary, but she hated always having to lie for her boss, so she quit. She then started working the third shift in a factory. She stayed there for nine months until she received a letter in the mail.

The train station in Chicago had informed her that they wanted to set up an interview with her. It couldn't have come at a better time for Rose and Glen.

Before Glen and Rose met, Glen had a one-night stand with a girl Gina. Gina became pregnant, claiming Glen to be the father. She kept calling, making Rose furious. She wanted Glen to pay child support, because she thought he was the father.

Glen told Rose that Gina had told him that she thought she was pregnant before they even slept together. Now, she changed the story.

Rose was upset because her ex, Jack, wouldn't give her the money he owed her from the divorce decree. It stated that if he were to remarry, that he would have to pay Rose $10,000.

Rose contacted her lawyer, and he got on Jack's case right away.

When God's timing is right in your life, you move. Especially if he wants you to be somewhere else.

When Rose found out she was hired, Glen moved to Indiana, to live with his mother and get away from Gina for awhile. She tried to press charges, but she was too late. Glen had already moved.

Rose sent $1,000 to Glen to put down on an apartment. When Rose came for a visit, Glen told her that he spent all the money. So Rose gave him another $1,000. When she went for her physical, he told her that he spent that money, too.

Rose thought that maybe he was paying off his credit cards, but that wasn't the case.

This irritated Rose. She decided to find an apartment the next time she was there and to put down the deposit herself.

They found a cozy apartment near the railroad tracks in a quiet little town. This way, Rose could ride the commuter train to work in case Glen wasn't able to bring her.

When Rose returned, she asked Kurt if he knew of anyone who could help her move. He did, so the moving was all set.

Incidentally, Kayla and Kurt gave birth to a darling little boy, Kyle.

14
Chicago

Rose moved everything on the fourteenth of March and reported to work on the seventeenth of March 1989.

Glen had lived in Chicago before, so he was able to find his way around. Just before Rose moved, Glen found a bartender job close to home.

When Rose first started with the train company, she had to go through six weeks of classes. During that time, Kayla had to go to classes in Chicago also. She rode the train to work with Rose. She stayed for a week. They had a wonderful time seeing the sights of Chicago.

Rose passed her classes with flying colors. Now she just needed to pass her physical, and she was all set to hop aboard.

Rose took her first trip to Saint Paul, Minnesota. It was a three-day run. When she returned, she went to the secretary of state to get her driver's license. When they asked her if she ever had a license before, she said no. They made her take a written test and a road test, which she passed with flying colors as well. Rose finally got a driver's license after six years without one.

Rose was off to a great start. She liked her job. It paid better than any waitress job she had. Almost triple.

Rose liked living in a quiet town, with the hustle and bustle all around her. There was a big Italian family across the street, so things were always going on next door.

One day, Rose was just coming in from New York, when she saw Glen standing in the train station with a red rose. He told her that this was a special day for her. He promised to take her out for supper later on in the day.

He took her to a fancy restaurant. There was an organist playing a beautiful three-tiered organ in the middle of the restaurant. Rose felt like Cinderella. Glen was very quiet as he waited for the right moment.

"Rose, will you marry me?"

Rose was in shock. She never thought that Glen would ever get up enough courage to ask her, but he did.

"Yes, Glen, I will marry you."

Glen was a decent man, always honest with her, so she thought. Rose respected him, but, she didn't like the way he always used his credit cards to pay for everything. This scared Rose. But she got over it when she saw the beautiful diamond that he bought her.

Rose picked out a dress, putting it in storage until the time was right for her to wear it.

When Rose and Glen moved into their apartment, Kerry was the landlord. She told them that if they wanted to decorate the apartment, they could. So Rose bought a Hawaiian wall mural for the living room wall. It fit perfectly with the decor. Rose bought covers for the seats and hung pictures throughout the rest of the apartment. She also hung curtains to match. It really was a cute apartment. It was cozy and warm.

The only thing Rose didn't like about her job was that she was on call all the time. Which meant that whenever she got home from a trip, she could be back on the train again twenty-four hours later bound for California,

New York, New Orleans, Texas, or wherever they wanted her to go. She had no say in the matter.

Glen hated it as much as Rose did, because they could never plan on anything.

The other thing Rose hated about her job was that she was the only white girl in her section of the train. The black men she worked with were always trying to get her in the sack with them. They didn't want to take no for an answer.

The sunrises and sunsets were picturesque beyond anyone's imagination. The mountains in Colorado were the same.

Rose caught a lot of beautiful scenery from the train.

One particular trip Rose will never forget. She was headed home from New York, when the train came to an abrupt halt. A man in the wheelchair had just committed suicide by way of the train. The train waited for the scene to be cleared before it started again. About ten miles down the track, it stopped again. This time it hit a small car, which wrapped around the engine, killing the man who went through the guard.

This made the train four hours late, so a complimentary dinner was served to three hundred people on board by the service attendants. Rose was dog-tired when they finally arrived in Chicago.

She had been sleeping for two hours that night, when Glen got home from work.

"Rose, wake up! I have something very important to tell you. I got a letter today stating that I need to go to Michigan to take a blood test for the baby that is supposedly mine."

"So what does that have to do with me?"

"You'll soon be my wife. It has everything to do with you."

"Glen, I'm tired. Please let me sleep. We can talk about this in the morning. I had a really bad trip."

"You don't care about me. All you care about is your stupid job."

"If you don't let me sleep, I'll call off the wedding."

"Maybe, that's best. You don't care about me anyways."

"Fine! The marriage plans are cancelled."

If only he would have let Rose sleep, they wouldn't have gotten into that argument. Things would have sounded different in the morning, when Rose was wide awake.

Rose cared for Glen, but he just didn't understand what she had gone through on her last trip. The marriage was called off. Rose wasn't about to change her mind. Rose didn't need all those problems in her life. She had enough to deal with.

The next morning, Rose was called in to stand by at the station in case someone called in sick. She hoped that she wouldn't have to take a trip that day.

She was lucky. She got to go home at five P.M. When she got home, she started packing up Glen's personal items. She called Glen, telling him she needed the car to go shopping.

She went down to the bar where he worked. She had a drink to calm her down. She went out to the car, opened the door, threw her car keys in the car, and locked it. Great. Just what she needed, to be locked out.

Glen wasn't going to give her his keys, but he saw her with a coat hanger in her hands. That was just what Rose had planned. She opened the door, took the house keys off Glen's key ring, locked the doors, and drove off, with Glen screaming at her for his keys. She pretended not to hear him.

She went home, packed the car with Glen's junk, then drove it back to the bar where he worked. She left the keys with the manager and drove away with the neighbors who followed her there.

Glen came by later on that night, but Rose wasn't about to let him in. She pretended she didn't hear him. He drove away then.

Glen had a place to live. He could go back to his mother's.

Glen made a mistake. He forgot to forward his mail. When his bank statement arrived, Rose opened it to find the $2,000 that he borrowed from her as down payment on an apartment. Rose was furious!

Because the phone bill was in his name, Rose told Glen that if he wanted his furniture back, he would have to pay the money back. Glen did for about two months, then he stopped.

Lucky for Glen he found out that he wasn't the father of the baby in Michigan after all.

Rose continued to work for the railroad, Glen moved back to Michigan.

Rose met Hope, who lived across the street and was sixty-eight years old. They became friends. Whenever, Rose had to go anywhere around town, Hope showed her the way.

Things were pretty smooth for awhile. Then Kerry sold the apartment building to a couple. They were friendly at first.

They remodeled the downstairs apartment first. It was in dire need of repair. Jenny and Rose became friends.

Rose bought a small car from a man whom the barber knew, so that she could go back and forth to Michigan to see her daughters and family.

Rose also received free passes for her daughters to take the train across country. During spring break, she took her daughters to Oakland, California. It was a mystery trip for Rose.

Rose wasn't aware that the time schedule had changed. She and the girls arrived at the train station an hour early, so they thought. Rose heard the conductor making the last call for their train. She still had to park the car before they could leave. The girls told the conductor to hold the train for their mother and he did.

Once on the train, the girls left their seats to check out the rest of the train. Rose stayed in her seat, listening to her head phones. She had a meditation tape on. She started talking silently with her Heavenly Father.

"Please, dear God, show me the way. Who is my soul mate?"

"I will show you your soul mate, Rose."

"I've been searching for my mate and can't seem to find him."

"Be patient, Rose. I will show you your mate during this trip."

"How will I know who he is?"

"Ask him his name."

Rose patiently waited. Then, she decided to check on the girls. She found them in the lounge car playing cards with some other children.

While Rose walked back to her seat, she noticed a man with shoulder-length hair, a beard, and a mustache in blue jeans and a pin-striped shirt, coming towards her. His sea-green eyes took her breath away. Her heart was pounding a mile a minute. She couldn't believe who she saw. Could it be her soul mate? The Lord was her soul mate?

"Dear Heavenly Father, is that who I think it is?"

"Ask him his name, Rose. You will see."
He walked into the lounge car to look at the scenery.
Rose went by him but didn't have the courage to ask him his name. She was still in shock.
Rose stood behind a seat by the doorway, so she could see him. He got up and entered the car that Rose was in. He walked past her, and Rose got up enough courage to ask.
"Excuse me." She tapped him on the shoulder. "Is your name Jes—"
Before she finished saying his name, he vanished into thin air. The man in the seat in front of her, saw the whole thing.
"I wouldn't have believed it if I didn't see it with my very own eyes," he said.
Rose was in shock. She couldn't believe what she had just seen, but it was true.
Normally, people with manic depression don't usually hear voices, but Rose did. The voice Rose first heard in her mind was the Heavenly Father's voice. Twice this had happened to Rose. Actually, it happened three times. The Bluegrass festival in the pines, the Indian at the Bluegrass festival with the key word, "love," and now on the train.
Rose didn't know why these events were happening to her, but they were.
These are events that you don't go around telling everyone about because they are liable to think you are crazy. But others had witnessed them, too.
The train ride was a great adventure for all three of them. They really had a great time seeing the countryside by train.
It cost Rose sixty dollars to get her car when they returned home. It was a good thing Rose had that much cash with her.

When Rose returned to her apartment, the loneliness set in. After Rose threw Glen out, she dated a few men from Chicago, but none of them liked her job.

So Rose began to write her book when she was alone. She sent a couple of chapters to American Friendly Publishers, but the only reply she got from them was a sweepstakes form in the mail. She also sent her chapters to Londervans, but they did not want to publish it because it wasn't a Christian book; so they thought.

Every time Rose would hear from American Friendly Publishers, she would write a little more. Even though, they wouldn't publish it, it was good therapy for Rose to get her frustrations out on paper. Since then, she has changed the whole format of the book.

For anyone who has suffered in the past, it is good therapy to write out their frustration, even if it is never sent anywhere. It eases the mind and soul. Throw out the junk from your mind.

Rose had been working on the train for almost a year. The time went by fast. She worked six days and was home for one day, then back on the train for six days. She had very little free time for herself, much less for her writing. Finally, when Rose couldn't take it anymore, she began to pray on her way to work. This was a four-day flip in Salt Lake, Utah.

"Dear Lord, I can't take it anymore. I'm tired of these long hauls. If you want me to write this book, then I will need money and the time off to write the book. There are three ways for me to get ahead: one. The train lottery, two. The Illinois lottery, or three. The American Friendly Publishers sweepstakes. Take your pick, but, if it's the train lottery, may there be no deaths."

Rose left it at that before she caught the train to Utah. On the way out, everything was fine. The service attendants were all in a cheerful mood. The train was on time, and the passengers were happy.

On the train coming back, the train was on time, whereas, the trains are usually late by three hours or more. There were passengers sixty-five and older, oxygen tanks, babies, including four-week-olds. The first day of the trip was fine. But not the second day.

The engineer missed a slow order to do thirty-five miles per hour. Instead, he was doing ninety miles per hour.

A couple that was seated in the very last car of the train asked if they could have lunch in the dining car. Rose told them that it would be okay. So they came in for lunch.

Everyone was seated in the dining car having lunch, when the train came to a screeching halt. The switch on the tracks split from the weight of the train. The lounge car jumped track, throwing the dining car to and fro before it stopped on its side. The nine cars following the dining car were twisted on opposite sides of the track, while the nine cars before the lounge car were perfectly intact, as if nothing were wrong at all.

Rose got caught in the pantry, dodging three urns as they came crashing to the floor, just missing her. Garbage was thrown all over the floor. Rose was hit in the back of the neck with a bottle of dressing and was left with a throbbing headache.

The other passengers were all right. Just a few minor injuries took place. The kitchen trap door was stuck shut. The side doors were twisted like a pretzel. No one could get through.

Just then, a gust of wind whirled through the dining car. Two men appeared in white suits at each doorway. They told everyone to remain calm, be seated, and fear not, that everything would be okay. With another gush of wind, they were gone.

George looked at Rose.

Where did those men come from? They couldn't have passed through the train," he said.

Rose just looked at George.

"Would you believe Heaven, George?"

"I believe, Rose."

The car where the couple was seated before they asked to be seated in the dining car was completely demolished. They would have been killed. There were 500 people on board, 100 injured, but no deaths.

George was able to get the trap door open to the kitchen. So they let the passengers from the dining car out that way.

The train landed in a cornfield, just outside Batavia, Iowa. It reminded Rose of the tiny farm town she grew up in, nothing but a pit stop with a handful of people to call it a town.

Within minutes, reporters were all around like bees to a hive. There were firemen, emergency units with juice and water, cop cars, buses, and helicopters flying overhead.

The townspeople had made sandwiches and provided juice and cookies for the passengers. The charter buses came in to provide transportation back to Chicago. It all happened so fast.

The minute Rose got off the bus in Chicago, the reporters were there to ask questions. Rose just ignored them as she headed inside the station. Once inside the station, the staff questioned Rose. She answered questions and told the staff that she was okay.

The next morning, Rose woke up stiff as a board. She made a doctor's appointment. Her left shoulder was five inches higher than her right. The doctor gave her some pain medicine.

On the drive home, with traffic backed up for miles, Rose's head got stuck to her left shoulder. Pain was throbbing down her back. She couldn't lift her head up for anything.

Good thing Jenny was painting at the apartment building when she arrived. Rose called the staff and told them what had happened. Jenny drove Rose to the emergency center at a local hospital, where they took X-rays of her. Then they drugged her with a pain reliever, and the doctor came in and snapped Rose's head back into place.

Rose was admitted for treatment. They took CAT scans and MRIs of her head and shoulders. She stayed for a couple of days, then they released her.

Because she had no feeling in her left arm, she went to a neurosurgeon for treatment. He poked around, but that was all.

Rose found a Japanese doctor, who used massage for treatment. After many sessions, he was able to release her hinged shoulder.

Rose went to the board to get some cash for being off from work due to injury. They gave her $200 a month to live on.

Rose hired a lawyer, thinking he could help her get the settlement she deserved, but he was of no use. She ended up firing him.

It was a good thing that Rose had her credit cards. At that time, Rose received a letter from American Friendly Publishers, stating that if she had the winning entry, she would win, ten million dollars. Rose didn't buy it at first, but then she heard a voice telling her that she had won.

The voice sounded the same as before when she had prayed. She thought it was an answer to prayer.

She was so excited that she went out to look at homes. She even put a bid on one, but someone else had a higher offer. She went around purchasing things for a new home. She bought a time-sharing condo package. And she also bought a new car.

Little did she know that if God can talk to you, so can Satan. Because Rose's judgment was poor, she wasn't able to tell the difference between the voices. This was the first time that Satan played tricks with her. And it wouldn't be the last.

Rose sank into a deep depression, so deep that she wanted to kill herself. She couldn't pay the rent, so the landlord was asking her for sexual favors.

She didn't have enough money for food, so she went to the sisters of a Catholic church. They fed her every week.

She met up with an Arabian gentleman who was very rich. He was sixty-nine, but Rose didn't care until he started playing games with her head. She moved in with him for a while, then moved back to her old apartment.

Rose found a homeless man who she moved into the attic to keep her safe from the landlord. He was just as poor as Rose, but at least he was company and he kept Rose from killing herself.

One night, a boy from across the road came to visit Rose. He asked her if she was a witch or something because of what she had seen in the past. She told him she wasn't a witch or anything like that. He asked her if she could find out something for him. He wanted to know if his friend was in Heaven or Hell. Rose told him that if she saw his friend, Kevin, she would let him know.

Rose had never done anything like that before. She didn't even know how to go about it. Then it came to her.

One morning, about five o'clock, Rose heard a knock on her kitchen door. The homeless man living with her at the time asked her if he should answer the door. Rose told him not to answer, in case it was the landlord.

Next, she heard little stones hitting her bedroom window. She looked outside and saw a rolling fog on the ground. There were two men standing there. One in all white and one in all black.

The one in all black was asking to speak to her.

"Rose, let me in! I need to talk to you."

"Who are you and why are you here?"

"I don't know who sent for me, but I need to come in and talk to you."

"Is your name Kevin?"

"I guess so. Why? Who wants to know?"

"I do."

The guy in white stood by the sidewalk as a lookout. He told the guy named Kevin that it was time to go. And with that, they vanished into thin air.

Since the Catholics believe in purgatory, Rose figured that's where he was at the time. If not, then he came from hell.

This was the first time Rose ever experienced anything like this.

Why Rose? Did she have a special connection or what?

Rose wasn't the only one who saw this happen; her friend, the homeless man, saw it also.

Rose sat down at night with a note pad to meditate. She thought she could write some thoughts on paper and then type them out.

Instead, Rose felt a presence leaning over her shoulder. So, she wrote, "hi."

"Hello," came back to her.

"Who are you?"

"Look inside the walls of the attic, and you will see."

Rose went up to the attic, where she found an eye chart, a brochure with W. F. Newcomb on it, and she also found a records book dated 1889.

"I understand you're a writer."

"Yes, that is correct. What can I do for you?"

"My time of death has not been recorded."

"It may be listed at the Archives, with Jesus Christ's saints."

"I will help you if you help me write my book."

"I promise I will."

Rose put the pad away and looked into it the next day. There was a church that had the Archives there. It was the church of the Jesus Christ Latter-Day Saints. Rose went there to see what she could find. They had no date of his death or how he died.

Next, Rose went to the Library of Congress in Chicago to see what she could find on microfilm. She waited and waited, but they wouldn't let her see the microfilm.

Rose found a small key hidden under the sink in the bathroom. They searched all over the house for a hidden treasure but couldn't find one.

Rose changed the locks to the apartment to keep the landlord away for awhile. He got so mad that he slashed the tires on Rose's car and bent the antenna.

Rose knew the landlord was coming, so she called the police. Rose told them that she wanted to kill herself. The cops brought her to a mental hospital.

Rose didn't receive treatment because she was pregnant when she went in. They took pregnancy tests and ultrasounds. The doctor told the nurse that they would look like seeds because it was only six weeks into the pregnancy. The nurse said, "Oh, like these, doctor?"

"Yes, just like those," the doctor replied.

When Rose got back to the ward, they gave her some medicine to drink. The following night, she was no longer pregnant. She was forced to drink the medicine.

"Rose, since you are not pregnant anymore, you must take this medicine."

Rose refused to take it. Since she signed herself in, she was free to go any time she liked. So she left.

When she got back home, her back door was cracked in half and her friend was nowhere around.

The landlord had bashed in the door while she was gone and threatened to kill her friend if he didn't leave.

This scared Rose. She couldn't move in with the Arabian. Her lawyer wasn't helping her in the least. Rose also got a letter from her ex, stating that he wanted more money for child support. She was tied up in knots with no place to run.

Finally, she went to the board, asking for her settlement. They gave her two choices: a lesser sum and still work for the railroad or a larger one and quit the railroad.

Rose decided to quit and take the larger sum. A man who wanted her to go to Texas with him took all her furniture. So her parents had hardly anything to move back home for her. Rose ended up in a different mental hospital, this time for a month.

Her parents got the money and paid off her bills while she was in the hospital. Rose was just drained by this tug-of-war.

Rose took the medication this time. At first, she felt like a walking zombie. But after awhile, she felt better.

Rose met a lot of interesting people. They all had problems of some sort. Some were worse than others. It was sort of like a prison, except there were no cells, just everyone locked up in one big room.

After a week, Rose got special privileges to go outside for breaks, and she was able to walk the grounds without supervision.

After the four weeks were up, her parents came and got her. The last thing Rose wanted was to do live with her parents. She was afraid of what her father might do. But he behaved himself.

15
Back Home

Rose was really depressed by it all. She enjoyed her job on the trains, but it was time she came back home to be with her children once again.

Rose saw an ad in the personal columns about a man who was seeking companionship. After three weeks, they agreed to meet each other for a church service. At first, Rose didn't know what to think. He had long hair, a mustache, and a really long beard. He seemed nice, but Rose was a little hesitant because of his looks.

His name was Barry. He lived in the country with his folks also. He told Rose that he had met her before. Then Rose remembered that when she worked at Brann's, the cook told her that a friend of his was interested in her. Rose had taken a peek at him in the hallway; he had his biker leathers on. She decided he was too wild for her, so she declined. Then he brought his whole family to Brann's and had her wait on them.

Rose didn't recognize him until he shaved off his beard and got a haircut.

Barry was wild back then, but he changed. Now, he was very religious. He had been studying to become a preacher. He was good, but he wasn't certified.

Rose had prayed before she met him, to meet up with a man who had the spirit of the Lord in him. She, too, was going through a change. No more hot and wild for Rose. She was ready for a change. Barry even talked as though he was the Lord sometimes.

Barry was good for Rose. He made her see a light in the very dark tunnel she was in. Rose contacted the church and told them that she needed to be baptized. She was baptized in a whirlpool. When the preacher's wife spoke in tongues, Rose knew that someone should interpret. The only thoughts that Rose had was *Yes, yes, it is true. This is Christ's bride.*

She wasn't thinking with a clear mind. In Revelations, it is revealed that Christ's bride is a church. But because Rose was having a grandiose notion, she believed it to be true. She left a note in her mother's Bible stating what she had heard in her mind.

Her mother looked at her.

"Rose, you must be sick. Are you sure you are taking your medication?"

Rose hated it when her mother said things like that. Why did her mother always think that she was sick, when Rose felt fine.

Her mother knew about the symptoms long before Rose did, but she never told Rose, who was left in the dark.

Rose met up with her friend, Linda, who wanted her to babysit for her kids. Rose was pleased to do it to get away from her parents for awhile. Linda didn't pay Rose, she just took advantage of her. Rose didn't mind. She just needed the break.

Since Rose thought she was going to marry a preacher, she started picking up religious material wherever she went.

In the spring of that year, Barry told Rose that he was moving up north. Rose asked if she could go with him, but Barry wouldn't let her.

Rose was disappointed. She wanted to get away from her parents, get married, and settle down. She was sick and tired of being single.

Kayla invited Rose to spend the weekend up north with her, Kurt, and Kyle in their cabin on a lake. It was just what Rose needed to break the blues. Kayla had been feeling the blues herself.

When Rose arrived, she noticed that Kurt was drinking a beer. He was always drinking beer. He never fell down or staggered around or slurred his words, he just always drank beer, one right after the other. This bothered Kayla, but she never complained about it. So Kurt just kept on drinking.

On Sunday, Rose went to the church that Barry had brought her to, thinking maybe he would be there, but he wasn't.

The preacher made a comment that night to pray to the Holy Spirit. Then he kept asking if the Holy Spirit was there. Rose got tired of his continual asking, so she prayed to the Holy Spirit. She asked the Holy Spirit if she could speak for the Holy Spirit to tell the preacher that the Holy Spirit was there. She waited for a response, then she heard it.

"Yes, Rose, you may tell him."

The preacher asked if anyone wanted to be touched by the Holy Spirit, so Rose came forward.

"Holy Spirit, are you present?" he asked again.

"Yes, I am here, saith the—" Rose answered.

Before she could finish her sentence, she was touched by the Holy Spirit. People in the audience probably thought she was the Holy Spirit by the way she answered. But that wasn't how it was meant to be.

On the way home that night, she also got a speeding ticket. Just what she needed.

Other than that, Rose had a nice weekend. She always had a great time with Kayla.

Easter rolled around, with the whole family gathering at her sister Sherry's house. Rose went to a Pentecostal church that morning, which got out kind of late. By the time Rose arrived, the family had already eaten lunch. This bothered Rose, but she wasn't planning on eating lunch with the family anyway. She had a bone to pick with her father after all these years; she finally had enough guts to face him. She warned her brother-in-law and her brother before she said anything, in case something should happen. Rose wasn't sure how her father would react.

"Daddy, what were you doing all those times you read the paper when I was in there taking a bath? Jacking off?

"And what about the time you showed me the facts of life? And all those times when I was a little girl that you made me sit on your lap so that you could feel up my dress?"

Her mother just buried her head and cried out loud. Her father's face turned red as a beet, but he didn't say anything.

The next thing Rose knew, her brother-in-law was escorting her out the door.

Rose went back to Linda's house for lunch. Things were peaceful until Linda told Rose that she could no longer stay with them.

Rose took her belongings and headed for Captain Joe's trailer. He was happy to see her. After he listened to her cry for help, he told her that she could stay for a couple of months. Rose was forever grateful. She gave him a big hug and said "thanks."

Rose collected all her police and hospital reports for her own viewing. She got them just in case she needed them for the book. Captain Joe paid for everything. He knew that Rose had traveled a rough road for a long time. At first, Rose just lay around. She didn't feel like looking for a new job. She just needed a break from it all.

Captain Joe always played cards on Wednesday night at a club. Joe invited Rose to go with him. At first, Rose stayed home, then one night, she decided to go just for the heck of it. Since Captain Joe was a senior citizen, most of his friends at the club were, too.

While Rose was there, she noticed a good-looking senior sitting all by himself drinking whiskey and coffee. How could he be so happy, when Rose was blue?

Rose liked the way he smiled at her. She got up enough courage to introduce herself.

"Hi! My name is Rose. What's your name?"

"My real name is Salvador, but my friends call me, Rex."

Rex and Rose had a certain ring to it.

16
My True Love

Time was running out for Rose once again. She had only a couple of weeks to find a place to live. Captain Joe wanted his freedom.

Rose prayed about this issue. She asked the Lord to show her her true love. Could it be Rex? Rose doubted it. He was at least twice her age, and she found out that he drank whiskey all the time, bottles and bottles of it. But why was he drinking so much whiskey?

"The reason I drink whiskey is because I lost my first wife nearly seven years ago. She was always on my mind. I thought if I drank enough whiskey, my time would be up and I could be reunited with her. It takes care of the loneliness I feel in my heart. She was a good woman, and now I've lost her. The good Lord took her away from me. Now I have no one to love."

"You have me, Rex." Rose couldn't believe that she actually said that. She was in shock.

"You seem very nice, Rose. I would like to spend more time getting to know you. Stop by my house tonight, and we will talk."

He got up and left before she had a chance to find out where he lived. She asked the bartender, and she told Rose where to find him.

Rose picked up a bottle of vodka before she found his place. If he was going to drink, so was she.

She found him sitting at the table, drinking his whiskey. Rose poured herself a drink and sat next to him.

Rose told Rex all about her past life and how rough it had been for her at times. Rex felt sorry for her. Rose told him that she planned on writing a book someday. He told her that he should write a book about his life as well. Then he began to tell her all about it.

"I've never seen my father. He died just before I was born. He had a coop full of chickens that he tended to. One night, there was some rustling going on inside the coop. My father took his bull whip with him, just in case. There he saw a rattlesnake coiled in the middle of the coop." His father snapped the head of the rattler off with his whip, but the head came flying through the air, landing with his fangs in his father's neck, killing him instantly.

"I don't remember what my mother looks like. She died, shortly after I was born, with a silver spoon stuck in her throat.

"I was raised by my sister, who had six other children to raise at the time. I wasn't allowed to eat with the family. I had to go outside and chip ice off the block for their drinks. When everyone was done eating, then I could come inside and eat the leftovers off the plates. This made me very angry. So mad, that I ran away from home just after my uncle died in his sleep. I was four years old at the time.

"I left Texas for good, never looking back as I ran. I made my own way by helping others along the way for something to eat and drink.

"As I grew older, I found sanctuary at police stations, where they gave me a place to sleep during the night.

"I never went to school. I taught myself how to read and write. When I was fourteen, I joined the army, but got booted out because I lied about my age. When I was old enough, I rejoined. I served in World War II and the Korean War, a total of fourteen years all together.

"I made it to Michigan and made Marie my wife. We were together for six months before I was drafted into the army. When I got out of the army, I became a plumber and also a furniture stripper.

"The house you see is the one I built by myself from the ground up. I did everything.

"I lost my step-daughter to alcoholism, and her husband died in a car crash. He died first. My step-daughter mourned his death, so she started drinking. She had sclerosis of the liver. And my wife died of old age. She was eighty-two when she died. She was twenty-five years older than me.

"Now I have nobody left. That's why I drink!"

Rose was impressed by his story. She felt sorry for him. No wonder he drank his sorrows away. No wonder he felt like ending it all.

The next thing she knew, Rex was asking her to marry him. She had only known him for three weeks. He was serious. He told Rose the only way she could move in was if they got married.

Rose needed time to think about this. Was he really her true love? He met all the check points on Rose's list, but he was an alcoholic!

"Dear Lord, I can be with Rex, except I can't stand the drinking. I will marry him if he quits drinking the whiskey."

She told Rex about her prayer.

"No problem," he said.

With that remark, he quit the whiskey, cold turkey.

Rose told him that if he wanted a beer or two once in a while, that would be okay. So that's what he did.

When the Lord wants things to happen, miracles happen.

He had been drinking whiskey day and night for seven years, and now for the love of a lady, he was willing to give it up without a fight. Yes, indeed, that's what he did. Rose was so proud of him. He was a completely different man when he wasn't drinking, full of love and compassion.

They got married on June 30, 1992. Rex was sixty-five, and Rose was thirty-two years old at the time.

When Rose told her mother that she was getting married to an older man, she was in shock. *It will never last,* thought her mother. Rose could read her thoughts. But Rose felt differently.

Her parents weren't invited to the wedding, but her friend, Kayla was asked to stand up. Kurt and Kayla were on their way when they lost the back axle to their car.

Rose and Rex had two witnesses from the courthouse stand up for them before the justice of the peace.

After the wedding, they made their way to the club for a small reception with a few friends.

A honeymoon was scheduled for a later date.

Just before they were married, Rex had to help Rose move her belongings from her parents' house. Her father just happened to be home that day. He wanted to have a few words with Rose before he handed over the money.

"Did you think that what I did to you while you were growing up was that bad?"

"Yes, Dad, I did. You invaded my privacy. You took away my youth. You destroyed the trust I had in you."

"I suppose you think I will burn in hell for what I did?"

"You will, Father, if you don't confess those sins before God."

"You almost caused a break up in my marriage! I deny everything!"

"That's okay, Dad. I'm not the one you have to answer to someday. Just remember, the Lord knows all things. He saw what you did. He also knows what you were thinking at the time. He knows everything. I suggest you confess before the Lord."

"I will not, because I haven't done anything wrong."

"It's okay, Father. When the time is right, you will know."

Rose felt sorry for her father. He was a good provider, but what he did to her was wrong, and she knew it. She forgave him, which made him all the madder.

Rose was told, as a little girl, to keep everything her father did to her a secret. She did until she was no longer a little girl.

He released the money and let her go. She was happy to be out of there.

Shortly after Rose and Rex were married, Rose started having problems. She couldn't make love to her husband because she considered him to be more like her grandfather than she did her husband. They slept in separate beds for awhile, until Rose was ready. Rex was very patient with her. He cared for her and treated her with tender loving care.

Rose repented of her sins and fasted for forty days and nights. She was deeply depressed with her whole life. Even though it was the illness that made her do the things she did, she still felt guilty.

Then came Christmas, with Rose's depression still lingering on. This time, she took sleeping pills, thirty-two to be exact.

Rex knew that she took them, and he began to cry. Rose typed out a letter to her girls and one to Kayla, bidding farewell. While she was typing, she could hear the Lord serenading her in the background. But, Satan was present, too. He kept asking Rose how many sleeping pills she took, and she would lie. The next thing she knew, Rose saw Satan's reflection in the window. He was laughing at her. Rose was too weak to defend herself, so she woke up her husband, telling him that she wanted to go to the hospital to get her stomach pumped.

When they arrived at the hospital, she was asked a bunch of questions about her experience and if she saw anything. They gave her some medicine to make her throw up. Then they gave her something to sooth her stomach.

After that, she was released. On the way home, Rose was very quiet. Rex didn't say much either.

Rose called a minister to pray for her. She felt as though she was demon possessed. Rose kept having a flashback of when she was a little girl. Her mother used to take the kids to a Pentecostal church every now and then. She remembered one time when the minister was casting out demons. He wore a black cape and had mysterious eyes. He told the parents in the audience to pray for their children to protect them from the demons. And that if they were vulnerable, the demons would enter in that child. Rose's mother took her kids out of the church. She told them to walk straight ahead and not to look back, but Rose looked back before she left.

Rose also heard the voices of demons in her mind. They wouldn't tell Rose which ones they were. Manic depression is filled with demons. Which ones? Inappropriate social behavior, inappropriate irritability, disconnected and racing thoughts, grandiose notions, poor judgment, suicide attempts, increased sexual desire, difficulty in concentrating, and remembering and making decisions, feelings of guilt, worthlessness, and helplessness.

At the time, Rose didn't know that those symptoms were a part of manic depression until later when she received the pamphlet.

Rose was just taking antidepressants for her illness. They weren't enough to put her on an even balance, so she started taking lithium. With it, she gained seventy-five pounds. Rose knew this would happen, but she didn't think it would happen right away. This made Rose even more depressed. She stuck with the program this time because she wanted to get better.

Rose took sleeping pills again. Only this time, she heard her youngest daughter crying at her funeral. It was just a grandiose notion she had, but it stopped her from committing suicide. Again she asked her husband to take her to the hospital, but the roads were so icy, they couldn't make it. Rex called an ambulance for her. She went alone.

When Rose arrived, they asked if her husband had been abusing her. Rose remembered a fight they had gotten into when he pushed her around a lot, so she told them that he had been abusing her.

Instead of going home, they made arrangements for her to go to a shelter for women. When she arrived at there, she met a black lady, Tinika. It just so happened that Tinika went to a morning Bible study just a block away. Rose told her that she was possessed with demons. Tinika invited Rose to go along so that they could pray for her.

At the Bible study, the ladies formed a circle around Rose, with Tinika in the middle, speaking in tongues.

Tinika told Rose to name the demons as they got cast out, so she did.

"Adultery, fornication, lying, stealing, abuse, and suicide."

Rose felt somewhat better after the session was over, but she sensed there were more demons inside her besides the ones that were cast out. Rose just didn't know what they were at the time.

Rex was worried about Rose, because the first three days she was there, they wouldn't let her talk to him. He didn't even know where she was at first. Until she told him. Then Kayla and Rex drove out together to see her. They brought her some cigarettes and some pop.

Tinika wanted Rose to go to church with her, so Rose told Rex that she wanted to stay a few more days.

At church, Rose gave her testimony, and many were impressed by her.

When she got back home, she went to see her therapist and psychologist. They asked her if she felt the need for hospitalization. Rose felt it was just a phase that she was going through, but that she was fine now. So they didn't hospitalize her.

Rose started reading her Bible on a daily basis. She ran across the unforgiveable sin and wanted to know exactly what that was. She called several ministers, but they wouldn't tell her what "blasphemy of the Holy Spirit" was. One secretary told Rose to read a verse in James in her Bible where it says that if anyone is sick, call for the elders of the church to pray for him and anoint his head with oil.

The only church that Rose found was the Church of Jesus Christ Latter-Day Saints that still anointed the head with oil and prayed over people who were sick.

Rose called the elders of the church to pray over her, and they anointed her head with oil.

Another thought that crossed Rose's mind was about the Trinity. The three-in-one could mean something totally different than what she was taught in Sunday school. Instead of looking at it like it was an egg, look at it as if it were a dictatorship. God being the president, Jesus Christ as the vice president, and the Holy Spirit (Ghost) as the secretary, in one unit.

It serves under one Godhead. This made a lot more sense than the egg theory.

Rose felt a lot of guilt over this, until the elders prayed for her. That's when she realized that it was her illness playing tricks on her. The Lord doesn't judge you when you are sick. He cares for the sick.

Rose asked her loved ones to forgive her for all she did to hurt them. They also asked forgiveness from Rose, except her father.

Rose started feeling much better about herself. She began sleeping with her husband. She found a job that she could handle. The medication was working for her. Rex found the pamphlet she needed to understand her illness: "Depression, What You Need To Know." Everything was going fine.

In order for Rose to get her company's insurance, she had to be off her medication for a year. She tried to do it, but she couldn't keep a handle on things.

She lost her job, which made Rose very depressed. It was so hard for her to find a job with her illness. People just did understand what it was.

She got laid off the same time American Friendly Publishers were notifying the winners by registered mail. She received a registered letter on a Saturday, over the Fourth of July, so she had to wait until Monday to get it. Rose thought for sure it was from American Friendly Publishers. She was so excited. She got the idea to open a shelter for the homeless people.

Rose started calling around to see just what it would take to get it started. The more she called, the more discouraged she became. Then Rose opened the registered letter. It was from her old company, informing her that she had been laid off.

Something was happening to Rose, but she couldn't put a finger on it. She woke up one morning and saw a pattern of a half moon made out of rose petals and leaves. Somehow, the papers on the desk had gotten wet. Rose lifted the papers and found a note written on the desk, which read, "Hllp U/SS/AA."

Rose thought for sure that they had received visitors during the night, but what kind of visitors were they? Was it the Lord and an angel, or was it an alien of some kind? Rose assumed that it was the Lord and an angel, but why? She didn't know why at first. Then she heard the voices in her mind.

"I have come to you to learn about your language."

"There are plenty of books in my drawing room, help yourself."

"Teach me how to read, by arranging the papers in a certain way on your kitchen table."

Rose arranged everything in perfect order that night before she went to bed.

The next day, Rose noticed one of her books on the shelve was misplaced. And the calculator on the table had been changed.

Rose started getting irritated with Rex because he didn't believe her. So she went on a day-long shopping spree. When she got home, she told Rex that she wanted a divorce. She wanted the truck, and he could have her car. Rose rode around town that evening, listening to the voices. She went where they took her.

Because Kayla went back to her religious roots, she no longer lived with Kurt. He went into rehab, and she and Kayla moved into a trailer by her parents' house. Rose stopped by.

Kayla had to go to work, but she told Rose that anything she needed was here. Rose took Kayla's swatch books with her. Before she left, she noticed a life-sized picture of a man in a tuxedo staring at her. She began to show him objects and explained what they were.

Rose journeyed to the beach, but it was closed. She almost ran out of gas, but the Lord was watching over her.

She returned home to Rex after he had called over and over. Rose's mother called. For some reason, she always sensed when Rose was having a grandiose episode. This made Rose even more irritable. She had to get away from those people. They were making her miserable.

Rose went in the living room to find her incense burner, but it was nowhere to be found. Rose looked at the picture of Jesus that she had by her desk and accused him of taking it. The picture began to cry tears of oil. Rex saw it also and couldn't believe his eyes. That was the first time it happened.

Rose had to get away, and left in her car. As she drove, the voices came back.

"Your husband killed your oldest daughter and her boyfriend. They came over for a bonfire. Rex pushed them in, then he tried to save them. Rex is okay, but your daughter and her boyfriend are in Hell."

Rose could hardly believe what had happened. Since she believed that the voice was the Lord's, it had to be true. But it wasn't the Lord's voice, it was Satan's.

Rose was in shock. How could Rex have killed her daughter? He was such a gentle and loving man. Certainly, he wasn't capable of this, or was he? If the Lord said it, then it had to be true. Satan loves to play games with people. He loves to tell lies.

Because poor judgment is also part of manic depression, Rose wasn't able to tell the difference between the voices she heard. They sounded the same to her, except for the lies. But Rose accepted the lies as truths.

She went to a chapel and cried her heart out. In the doorway of this chapel, she saw an Indian poking his head out the door. While in her car, she talked to this Indian. After she was through telling her story, she walked up to the chapel doors, but there was no one there. Everything was locked up.

Next, Rose followed the flowers along the roadside to a golf course. The voice told her that was where her other daughter had been killed. She was caught in a big meat pressure cabinet roasting like a stuffed pig. Rose tried to get the cabinet open, but it was locked.

Rose was overwhelmed with grief. How could they do this to her children?

She stopped at a gas station, when the cops arrived. They held Rose there until her husband arrived. Rose was fuming.

"You murderer! You killed my daughter! Get away from me!

"Rose, I did no such thing!"

The next thing Rose knew, she was being taken away by ambulance to a hospital for treatment. At first, she was under observation for twenty-four hours. After that, she was allowed to join the group. After the first week, she was still groggy. She was more herself during the second week. Her lithium level was very low when she arrived. So, they increased her level and gave her Haldol for the voices.

Rose called Rex to apologize for all the trouble she caused him. He accepted her apology. With that, he made his way up to see her. He was there everyday until she was released two weeks later.

Rose knew that he still cared for her dearly. She could see it in his eyes.

Rose made a lot of new friends during her stay. When she was ready to leave, they gave her presents and bid her farewell.

July 1993 was the last time Rose was in the hospital for manic depression.

With Rex's tender loving care, Rose would have gotten worse instead of better.

During Easter the following year, Rose went to see an Easter play called: "He Lives." It was all about Jesus Christ's life, death, and ascension. The man who played Jesus looked and acted just like him. When Jesus ascended, he wore a white robe with a navy blue sash on his shoulder. After he ascended, the townspeople, dressed in robes, said their farewells. What caught Rose's eye, was the short elderly gentleman with gray curly hair, clean-shaven, standing in the same white robe with a navy blue sash, waving to the people.

When Rose drove to the play, she heard a voice.

"Rose, I have a surprise for you today. Just watch and you will see."

Since Rose started using Haldol, she has been able to use better judgment in discerning the voices that she hears. She made up a code to be able to tell them apart.

God calls her "Rose," the Lord Jesus says, "Aloha, pretty lady," and Satan says, "Aloha, pretty baby."

When Satan tries to get hold of Rose, she ignores him. She has nothing to do with him anymore.

Rose walked up to the stage where God was standing.

"I know who you are! You're—"

Before she could get out the name, the man looked at her, holding a finger of silence to his lips. Rose just smiled and walked away. She got her ticket stubs autographed by the man who played Jesus.

Rose went to the same play with Rex the following year but didn't see the short, curly-haired guy at all.

Since then, Kayla and Kurt set a wedding day in December 1996. Rose's two daughters still live with her ex. Rose was never able to get enough money to raise her daughters, but she did manage to write the book she always said she was going to.

Now that the storm clouds have rolled away, she will have happiness forever.